Peter Alliss's
SUPREME CHAMPIONS
OF GOLF

Peter Alliss's
SUPREME CHAMPIONS
OF GOLF

CHARLES SCRIBNER'S SONS
New York

LIBRARY OF CONGRESS CATALOGING-IN-PUBLICATION DATA

Alliss, Peter
The supreme champions
1. Golfers – Biography.   I. Hobbs, Michael, 1934–
II. Title
GV964.A1A437   1986   796.352′092′2[B]   85-30259
ISBN 0-684-18320-X

1 3 5 7 9 11 13 15 17 19   20 18 16 14 12 10 8 6 4 2

Made and printed in Great Britain by
William Collins Sons & Co. Ltd, Glasgow

CONTENTS

Photographic Acknowledgements

The authors and publishers are grateful to the following for their help in supplying photographs and for allowing their copyright pictures to be used:

Allsport Photography pages 31, 129, 139, 193; Associated Press pages 30, 33, 80; BBC Hulton Picture Library pages 14, 40, 102; Peter Dazeley pages 72, 184, 185; Lawrence Levy pages 167, 181, 195; H. W. Neale pages 62, 73, 83, 85, 92, 97, 101, 114, 118, 123, 126, 127, 136, 150, 156, 168, 180; Popperfoto pages 50, 57, 59, 95; Phil Sheldon pages 57, 112, 145, 161, 170, 174, 189; US Golf Association pages 16, 17, 19, 28, 45, 47, 61, 67, 70, 71, 77, 96, 104, 111, 134, 143, 149.

INTRODUCTION

For many years I have been fascinated by the question of what makes a Supreme Champion. I've followed the exciting careers of many Supremes from a variety of sports, including my own sport of golf, in spite of some of them being 30 years older than myself. My first recollection of a true great was Gordon Richards, now Sir Gordon, and still sprightly well into his eighties. There followed the footballers Stanley Matthews and Tom Finney, two names that caused equal delight and frustration among both their followers and those who downgraded their efforts. There was Fred Perry, who had three victories at Wimbledon and who still to this day wears a mantle of greatness. There was also Sir Malcolm Campbell and his world speed records on four wheels, and various other players of sports who are set apart from the rest such as Babe Ruth, Mark Spitz, Joe Davis, Carl Lewis, Bjorn Borg and Martina Navratilova.

I've always made my own sort of order of merit of players which has been, quite naturally I suppose, confined to the game of golf. There have been the good players, the very good players, the champions and the Supreme Champions. I've always felt that there must be some common denominator running through them all, which becomes more evident the higher up the scale you go, that made them want championships, victory, success, power and adulation more than most. It's very easy to say that to be a Supreme Champion you must have dedication, balance, flair, touch, nerve, good health and probably a dozen other qualities too but by themselves they don't suffice. Very often there's a little bit of magic missing. In this computer age, it ought to be easy to feed in all the necessary data and within seconds be told what makes a truly Supreme Champion. But I don't think it's like that at all, because some Supremes seem to have more luck than others even though the saying 'You make your own luck' is still valid.

Some years ago I was making a television series in which I was comparing old champions with their new counterparts, and I did an interview with Sir Gordon Richards at his home in Wiltshire. After we'd finished the programme we were sitting having a cup of coffee and I asked him what one ingredient, if he could pass it on, would he choose for a young horseman or woman coming up today? He paused a few moments and, while he was thinking, I thought, 'He's going to say balance, timing, the judge of a good bit of horseflesh, a rapport with the animal, lack of injuries or no problem with weight or diet (for he had moments before told me that, although he hadn't ridden a race for some 30 years, his weight was still exactly the same as it had been throughout his entire career). Eventually, however, the great man cleared his throat and said one word: 'Desire'.

Well, a good answer but I don't necessarily think it encapsulates the whole reason why certain people become Supremes. I've known plenty of people with desire who've applied themselves. How many professional and amateur golfers in my time, both men and women, have I seen standing on the practice ground for hundreds of hours in the rain and shine, practising this shot and that in an effort to perfect their game. But that magic ingredient was always missing. There have been players who have won more than a share of tournaments but never, even with the dedication to practise of a Ben Hogan, Gary Player or Seve Ballesteros, managed to reach the greatest heights.

Thus desire isn't enough, practice isn't enough and skill isn't enough unless you have the nerve. Some might argue that the Supreme Champion must have the best technique or be the most prolific tournament winner; I agree that these are yardsticks of a sort but they're not ones that I think are definitive. One might look at the players who have won the most money and in modern times few can beat the records for being pure money-machines set by Billy Casper, Curtis Strange and a new up-and-coming player in the United States, Corey Pavin, but though Billy Casper won a few major events, somehow or other he never quite made the rank of Supreme Champion but he came as close as anyone.

So my choice has been based on players' performances in the world's major golfing events, the British Open Championship, the US Open, Masters and PGA. The Tournament Players' Championship, which is held annually on the new magnificent Players' Course in Florida, and the Canadian Open Championship, which is a lot older than the PGA Championship, have good claims either to ease out the US PGA or to bring the total number of major golfing events to five or six.

But what would happen, I hear you cry, should the Australian Open Championship take off in the next ten or twelve years? Similarly the growth of golf in Japan has been enormous and perhaps one day there will be a Tokyo or Japanese Open which will rival anything we've seen in previous years. You see, though I'm a great traditionalist, longevity isn't really the be-all and end-all of everything, and one must be prepared for some change, but at the moment our Supreme Champions must be selected, on my scorecard at least, on the basis of how they have performed in those four major championships; and I also include the British and American Amateur Championships. True, they have dwindled in stature and are sometimes considered no more than stepping-stones to the professional arena. This means that the fields are not quite as 'known' as they were in the past, though the quality of the players is, certainly on the American scene, very high indeed. But the sad thing, for supporters of amateur golf, is that not many competitors playing in the Amateur Championships are over the age of 24. Once they have shown their prowess they scuttle off to try to win fame and fortune in the professional ranks. So the long-term amateur, such as Jay Sigel or Joe Carr, whose career you could follow with great interest for a number of years has now almost entirely disappeared. On today's amateur front a Scott Verplank, a Philip Parkin or José Olazabal almost inevitably leaves the amateur stage as soon as he feels his game is ready for the professional circuit or when he finds the right manager who can get him contracts worth $250,000 a year before he plays a serious professional stroke. There is therefore no longer a tradition of the great players continuing in the amateur game and for that I shed a tear.

In the past, however, very few amateurs turned professional, so those championships were almost as difficult to win as the four major professional championships of today. The other side of the coin is that the US Masters Championship hasn't always been a major in the world of golf. After all, it had fairly humble beginnings back in the early 1930s; though it was started by some great characters including the greatest golfer of his day: Bobby Jones. But it was set up primarily as a meeting-place for professional friends to be invited to play golf. The date was even arranged to coincide with the sports writers travelling between New York and Florida. They somehow managed to have a week off in between the training schedules for the various baseball teams which would soon dominate the summer on the sports pages of American newspapers.

It wasn't really until the early 1950s that the Masters took off, which it did for a variety of reasons including the emotive influence and presence of Bobby Jones, who was at that time beginning to suffer from the terrible disease of syringomyelia, and the advent of General Eisenhower, one of the most popular American figures on both the political and sporting scene, who had a cottage at Augusta. How often did we see pictures of Eisenhower pottering round Augusta in a golfcart, playing modest golf but enjoying it tremendously. In his own way Eisenhower did as much to popularize the Masters, its setting and its mystique as Arnold Palmer, who was the first great hero of Atlanta.

You see, the four major championships are all very different, and to win in both the United States and in Britain demands different techniques, skills and certainly patience and nerve. Bernhard Langer from West Germany put it very well after winning the 1985 Masters when he said: 'The pressure was of a very different kind; different to anything I've ever suffered in any other tournament.'

That's what winning major championships is all about: the pressure is different. It's extraordinary how few players have ever scored a birdie on the final hole to win a championship. Many times players have taken a one-over-par to win a championship as Andy North did in both his US Opens. For others there has been a slight stumble, a hiccup and sometimes the championship has been secured with a very bravely holed putt for a par. The mental pressures, the noise, the awesome setting and the huge rewards all combine to unsettle you. As Bobby Jones said 60 years ago, 'Only championships count'. Well, that may have been particularly true for an amateur player but one mustn't put down the professionals who see playing as a way of making money. They'll settle for a place in the Top Ten, accumulating dollars along the way and, if you look down the American list of money-winners, certainly over the last five or six years, you'll see players who perhaps haven't won a single event during the year yet have taken home $300,000. Money-making machines they are indeed.

I make no apology for giving full credit to amateur championship victories and indeed rate them considerably higher than the routine amassing of money in professional tournaments. In the case of Jack Nicklaus, whose career has spanned more than 25 years, we always – I think rightly – count in among his 19 major wins his two US Amateur Championships. Yet we often forget the same achievements in the case of lesser players such as Lanny Wadkins, Craig Stadler or Jerry Pate. But, on the other hand, nobody in this hard and cruel age would contemplate putting Jay Sigel, who won the US Amateur Championship in both 1982 and 1983, in our category of Supreme Champions. However, he deserves special mention because he is a true-blue amateur, refusing to accept any monetary inducements to play at amateur level the game he loves. There are no hidden boxes of golfballs stuck here, nor air tickets secreted in the jacket pocket to get him from A to B. He is quite prepared to pay his own way: a remarkable animal indeed in this hard, commercial world.

The competitive programmes, the scheduling of the giants of the game, such as Hagen, Jones, Nicklaus, Watson, Ballesteros, Langer and others, clearly show that they place enormous importance on each of the four major events that we've already spoken about, as well as the TPC and, increasingly today the Canadian Open. Each one of them tries to organize his year around those four or six dates, which begin with the Masters in April and end with the US PGA Championship in mid-August. Many other events, of course, are prestigious; there are the championships of Europe, the British Masters and PGA Championships but one feels that the great players treat those events almost like very superior practice rounds, in spite of the added kudos if they win. But if these great names did in fact treat many events as just superior practice rounds, they were certainly just as effective in what one might call these ordinary tournaments, with perhaps the exception of Bobby Jones who hadn't the time as an amateur to play in many events. Indeed, when we look at his playing career it's quite extraordinary how little competitive golf he actually played.

What conclusions can we draw from looking at our Supreme Champions? Snead, Hogan, Nelson, Palmer and Nicklaus were the most prolific winners on the US Tour. Locke, Thomson, Player and Ballesteros reign supreme as international competitors. Henry Cotton and Seve Ballesteros during their best years were and are always firm favourites to win every tournament on the European scene. What made these men great players?

Was there a common denominator? Some had backgrounds of poverty, while others came from the middle classes. Nearly all started out just trying to make a living. Early on, however, something in them or someone spurred them on and suddenly made them aware that they could be great players. A few – Jones, Hogan, Nicklaus, Watson, Ballesteros – certainly have, or had, even higher ambitions. They had the urge to be the greatest of their own or any other time.

Another fascinating feature of our champions is the way they actually played the game. To the trained eye almost every one of our 15 has what would appear to be serious flaws in their basic golf swing. Others had distinct playing weaknesses such as Walter Hagen's wildness from the tee but, as my father said of him, he never hit two bad shots in a row. With Arnold Palmer, it was relatively poor pitching and Bobby Jones was no more than adequate when it came to precision play from bunkers – the same could be said of Jack Nicklaus and Bobby Locke. Almost the only common factors in playing ability are that each was a long enough hitter and at least a good enough putter in their best years. Someone of course always had the edge over the others in one or two departments of the game. Nobody ever putted better than Locke, played better bunker shots than Player, and hit the ball straighter than Hogan. Perhaps when the final roll call is made some higher judge may decree that the neglected Byron Nelson was, after all, the greatest of them all, lacking only the ambition and drive to grind away year after year.

However, much more than playing ability and skill and style and even ambition, I believe that nerve is the vital factor. In golf there is too much time to think of the consequences of each shot. For many, the glittering prizes which reward success and the fear of throwing a championship away with just one error can bewilder the mind and unsettle you completely. Peter Thomson, many years ago when we were sitting on a plane, said that the tighter the situation became for him in classic championship play, the clearer things were. His mind became sharper and his view of the shot brighter. Everything became calm and he saw exactly what he had to do. In other words, he felt completely in charge of the situation. I don't think I ever saw Thomson lose a championship, or a tournament, that he should have won – and that surely is a hallmark of a Supreme Champion. That's not to say that the Supreme Champions don't suffer like anyone else, but overall they manage to control their feelings, dismiss negative thoughts and concentrate totally on the job in hand: victory. Trevino certainly has nerve; how often have I seen him at the crucial moment about to strike the ball, while aware of the crowd still moving and talking, pull the shutter down and concentrate all his efforts on that single shot which is only going to take a second or two. There are indeed very few players who are capable of doing that.

So, I have chosen my men, whose deeds stretch over a span of some 70 years. With the exceptions of Hagen and Jones where I relied on their records and my father's recollections, each is a player I have watched and analysed myself. Some will perhaps be surprised by the omission of such names as Billy Casper, Johnny Miller, Tony Jacklin and Cary Middlecoff. Certainly players of the future who may one day qualify as Supremes include Bernhard Langer, Hal Sutton and others not yet recognized by either experts or the public. But the main careers of the Caspers and Millers are over while the Langers and Suttons still have far to go. In both these instances their major championship records have ruled them out – if only just. I must admit, though, that there are four omissions more glaringly obvious than the ones already mentioned: Young Tom Morris, J. H. Taylor, Harry Vardon, James Braid and perhaps Willie Anderson. Each is almost certainly a man who would have made his mark on any age. Their playing careers, however, took place before I was born and before my father, Percy Alliss, embarked on his career. Yet each had four or more victories in the major championships of the day and I salute them.

And now, I must begin with Walter Hagen. I could hardly have a better man to start me off.

WALTER
HAGEN

Walter Hagen is the only one of my Supreme Champions that I neither saw play nor met. Indeed, I was born in 1931 when he was no longer the best player in the world; having won his last major Championship in 1929. Yet Hagen's was a name that resounded throughout my youth. My father, Percy, had lost to him in a play-off for the 1931 Canadian Open in the year of my birth and had competed with and talked to him many times. That Canadian Open was one of Walter's last big wins and in some ways typical of him.

With some of the field still out on the course, Hagen decided his total of 292 was good enough to win and began to celebrate. But he hadn't bargained on the storming finish my father produced, 3s on each of the last five holes with a putt of some 30 feet holed across the final green to equal Hagen's total. There was a 36-hole play-off and when they finished level, out they went again for a sudden death, my father giving way on the 37th hole. I remember so well one of my father's comments on Walter's play: 'He never hit two bad shots in a row.' This says something about Hagen the man. He was renowned for playing more bad shots than you'd believe of a great player but was tremendously resilient and unperturbed by disaster. After a wild slice into the rough, or a half-topped iron shot into a bunker, he seemed to relish the challenge of making good the damage and, so legend would have us believe, usually did.

Walter Hagen (right) playing an exhibition match with my father, Percy Alliss, at Wannsee Golf Club in Berlin in the early 1930s

By coincidence, the Canadian Open had also been the scene of Hagen's début in tournament golf in 1912. Asked how he had done when he returned to his home club, Hagen had replied: 'I lost'. Even then, golf to Hagen was all about winning, so he didn't consider his eleventh-place finish, though honourable, worth a mention. His next appearance was in the 1913 US Open at Brookline Country Club in Massachussetts. To his fellow pros, Hagen bouncily announced himself by saying, 'I've come to help you boys take care of Vardon and Ray.' These were Harry Vardon (who had won the US Open some years before and eventually won six British Opens) and Ted Ray, holder of the British Open title and a future US Open Champion. Everyone thought that one of the two would win.

After three rounds, Hagen was just two strokes behind the leaders but began his final round disastrously: 6, 5, 7. However, he had watched Harry Vardon in practice and much admired his easy, flowing swing. He decided, as things could hardly get worse, to imitate it. There was a dramatic improvement, an eagle followed by a couple of birdies, which made up the lost ground.

Well there was a fairy-tale ending to this championship but it didn't concern Walter Hagen. An unknown amateur, 20-year-old Francis Ouimet, tied with the two Englishmen and beat them in a play-off, thus launching a golf boom in the United States. Hagen, going all out for victory, topped a brassie shot from a poor lie and later hooked a long-iron. His tie for fourth place went unnoticed because of the euphoria over Ouimet's victory.

The following year at Midlothian, Illinois, Ouimet opened up with a 69, one of the first rounds below 70 ever played in the championship. Hagen didn't want to compete. He was in agony from food poisoning. However, his expenses had been paid and he felt he could hardly return home without putting on a show. His driving was awful; his recoveries and putting superb. It all added up to a 68, which equalled the championship record. Although his scoring was not as good as the effects of food poisoning wore off, his four-round total of 290 equalled the US Open record. Walter Hagen from Rochester, New York, had arrived at the age of 21.

Walter Hagen was one of the five children of William and Louise Hagen who were both of German immigrant extraction. He was introduced to golf at the age of eight by caddying for 10 cents an hour. Even at that age, he soon discovered what he considered the secret of putting: controlling the stroke with the last two fingers of the left hand. His parents did nothing to encourage his golf and I expect they would have thought it no way to make a living for the game was virtually unknown in the States. No one could have guessed Walter would make a fortune from it. Why should they have? After all, he was the first to do so.

His father, a blacksmith in carbody shops, was to learn quite early that there was money in golf. At nineteen, after five years as assistant, Walter

The young Hagen before he hit the fashion scene

was appointed club pro at Rochester for the princely sum of $1,200 for an eight-month season. He was also able to get his father the greenkeeping job, despite his unlikely blacksmith's pedigree. Even so, William Hagen didn't watch his son play competitive golf until 1931. His mother never did.

Hagen himself didn't think being US Open Champion any great thing. Was it, he wondered, even his best game? He was offered a baseball try-out for the famous Philadelphia Phillies and turned it down, after much thought, mainly because golf was a game for individuals and Walter felt he'd found his niche. After all, he'd reached the top so effortlessly in golf that there was a chance he could do the same at any other sport. Of course, in his early years he practised, though he would probably have denied it. Hagen seems mainly to have picked up the game by playing at Rochester and observing how others played their shots. Years later, he was to be amazed at how much work his successors put in on the practice grounds.

Watching Byron Nelson going through his strenuous routine, he said: 'What a shame to waste all those good shots. That's nothing but corporal punishment.' Hagen also remarked that such intensity could ruin confidence – 'I'd be afraid of finding out what I was doing wrong.' So, with little practice and no teacher, Hagen developed a good swing – whatever some experts might say. Like Nicklaus, his head was turned away from the ball as he started the clubhead back, in almost a one-piece movement, though he did leave the clubhead behind for a split second. His stance, however, was very wide, about double his shoulder width, and this led to a tendency to sway on the backswing. This was full, with the club taken a little past horizontal. Perfectionists might say that he rose too much on his left toe at the top of the backswing but his hip turn of only 45 degrees was far ahead of his time. Hagen himself declared that he began with a sway and ended with a lurch, both probably a result of that very wide stance. The lurch, however, came after the hitting area. Everything was correct when clubhead met ball. Most important of all, he had rhythm and balance, though the latter sometimes gave way at the end of the follow-through.

Hagen featured little in the next two US Opens but picked up a tournament here and there. He had won seven of the few events played by the time the 1919 US Open came to Brae Burn in Massachusetts after a two-year gap brought about by the First World War. He began with a

The stance is too wide, left-hand grip too strong, left arm a little bent and the ball absurdly far back, but Hagen won more major professional championships than anyone until Jack Nicklaus

78, not good by any means, but not as bad as it sounds, if you take into account relatively poor equipment, uncut rough, unraked bunkers and unmanicured greens.

When the last round began, he was five strokes behind the leader, Mike Brady, the clear favourite, who finished with an 80. As he came to the last hole, Hagen knew what he had to do to tie and produced the first of his legendary bits of gamesmanship. Hagen had an 8-foot putt to equal Brady's total. He paused awhile, requesting that his opponent be summoned from the clubhouse to watch him hole it. He was and he did.

If Hagen had intended that Brady should be demoralized for the play-off, it didn't work out too well. It was neck and neck all the way. Then Hagen tried another ploy to undermine his opponent's confidence:

'Mike,' he said, 'if I were you I'd roll your shirt sleeves down.'

'Why?' said Brady.

'All the gallery will see your muscles quivering.'

On the 17th hole, Hagen found his ball embedded in mud. He called for a ruling, in the hope of a free drop. Officials refused this, so Hagen announced he was by no means sure it was his ball. He'd have to identify it. This involved moving the ball and, at the end of the process, his lie was far more playable. He won by a stroke.

Hagen had now won the US Open twice. It was time to see if he could be world champion, so across the Atlantic he went to compete in the first post-war British Open at Deal, in Kent. With him, he took 12 colour-co-ordinated golf outfits and his by now famed black and white shoes. (He had decided that snappy dressing was part of professional golf several years before, when he'd been highly impressed by one competitor's attire of white silk shirt, white flannels, red bandanna, white buckskin shoes, all topped off with a plaid cap.)

For the British Open, Hagen added an Austro-Daimler limousine and a footman. But when he arrived in such opulent style, the secretary refused him entry into the clubhouse to change. After all, wasn't this American chap a professional? 'You can change your shoes in the professional's shop,' he said. I think Hagen relished the situation and his behaviour in the championship certainly embarrassed that secretary. If he wasn't allowed to use the clubhouse, there was no embargo on the car park, but professionals of the day didn't own cars. Hagen parked his Austro-Daimler in front of the clubhouse windows and daily had his footman serve him lunch there with appropriate wines. The members didn't like it at all.

Sadly, his style off the course wasn't equalled by his golf. All sorts of stories have gone the rounds over the years, two particular old chestnuts being that Walter didn't once break 80 in the championship and finished 53rd out of 54 qualifiers.

It's a case of imagination trying to improve on the facts. They were bad enough. Hagen went out in his first round in about level par and then only just broke 50 on the way back. However, Walter's 84 wasn't much worse

Abe Mitchell and Walter Hagen posing for the camera during a challenge match. Mitchell is dressed in the style of Vardon, Taylor and Braid; Hagen is much more casual but still elegant

than the eventual champion's opening 80. But George Duncan was to improve greatly, his last two rounds being 71 and 72, while Hagen's were 78 and 85. So he did break 80 and he wasn't 53rd out of 54. There was one golfer, a certain Bob Mackenzie from Stanmore in Middlesex, an early mentor of my father's, who used up 361 strokes. At least Hagen beat that by 42 and of course there were many other players between them. In fact, he hadn't done all that badly on his first appearance in the championship – 26 strokes behind the winner was a little better than Jack Nicklaus managed on his first championship appearance in 1962!

Hagen showed what he was made of a couple of weeks later when he won the French Open at La Boulie. He decided he liked Britain and Europe and would return. His failure at Deal he put down to his lack of one shot: the low pitch and run. Hagen was a master of the high pitch shot but these had been blown away on the wind. It would, he vowed, be very different on his next trip.

So it was. At St Andrews in 1921, Hagen broke 80 in each round and, in the morning's play on the final day, had one of the lowest rounds that year. It was a 72 which put him a stroke ahead of Jock Hutchison and level with Roger Wethered, the players who were to tie for the championship later that day. They finished in 70 and 71 while Hagen took 77. However, he'd nearly got the hang of links golf as his performances over the next three years were to show. At Royal St George's, Sandwich, in 1922 he became the first American-born player to win. Scoring was high and Hagen came from behind with one of the lowest rounds of the championship, a 72. This was the year of one of the greatest forlorn pursuits that the championship has ever seen. With Hagen apparently the winner, the whisper went round that George Duncan was playing the round of his lifetime. Four strokes behind Walter, he was racing along at his usual gallop with birdies in full flow. He came to the last, a very difficult hole, needing a par-4 to tie and put his second shot just short of the green. In as little time as it takes to read this, he pitched short, glanced at the line of his putt – and missed it.

At the presentation, Walter eyed his cheque, was not too impressed at a row of noughts being absent and handed it straight to his caddie. There was to be another incident at the presentation the following year. It continued to rankle with Hagen that professionals were not allowed into the clubhouse. It was all very different from his club in Florida where he was soon to be professional and its President as well! In 1923 after three steady rounds, Arthur Havers held on to beat Walter by a stroke. The presentation was to be made inside and the committee decided to be broad-minded and invited Hagen to attend. He did not accept, made a short speech to the crowd and invited them along to join him for a drink at a local pub.

Another good year for Hagen was in 1924. Conditions were difficult, with quite strong winds throughout. There were very few scores under 75 and with a round to go Hagen and E. R. Whitcombe were level. The Englishman set out first. His closing round of 78 may seem poor today but remember the days of low scoring had not yet arrived. In fact, Whitcombe's score seemed likely to win when it was heard that Hagen was out in 41, with Hoylake's very testing closing holes still to play. He had to come back in 36 to win. Hagen buckled to his task, his long game in the wind was at its best and the occasional good putt went in. He finally needed a 7-foot putt for victory and knocked it into the middle, his wife rushing onto the green to embrace him.

Hagen had married Margaret Johnson in 1917, a woman who enjoyed a lively social life and this suited Hagen very well indeed. A year later, his only child, Walter Junior was born. The marriage didn't last long, however, and it was another lady, the former Edna Strauss, who caused the stir by racing onto Hoylake's 18th green. Hagen was just not suited to married life. He liked to travel and to attend or give parties. It is said that he didn't really own a home until he finally retired from golf. Hagen, remember, was not a traveller in the same way as today's stars who jet around the world to a tournament and then fly back home, or onwards to another. Hagen was away for months on end giving exhibitions and taking the gate money away in a suitcase – and then spending it. In 1930 he set sail on a world tour with Joe Kirkwood, a very good golfer who was ideally suited to exhibitions because he was the greatest trick shot artist of the day. They went all over Australia, New Zealand and Japan with many other ports of call.

In 1937 he was even more ambitious. Again with Joe Kirkwood, they toured for no less than 18 months. As Hagen put it: 'We played just enough golf to take us where we wanted to go.' Starting with the Pacific Islands, they visited Australia and New Zealand again and then went on to India, Aden and France before arriving in Britain to play in the Open. Hagen stayed on for a few months playing exhibitions in Europe before visiting several African countries for the big game hunting. There was more of that to follow in Ceylon and India, where he shot with the Rajah of Calcutta. Onwards Kirkwood and Hagen continued through Malaya, Java, Hong Kong, even China, before Japan was the last stop.

Exhibitions were indeed perhaps the main reason why Walter Hagen was interested in winning major championships. He always liked to hold one as it improved his billing. His fee was $75 after his first US Open win but rose to $300 after the First World War. However, Walter preferred to take the gate money. Hagen missed the 1925 British Open because, it was said, he'd decided to give the others a chance, but he turned up at Royal Lytham again in 1926. He began magnificently with a 68 but fell away later. Yet he thought he was still in with a chance when he reached the last hole, which was then 378 yards. It was a 2 to tie. For his medium-iron to the green he demanded that the flag be removed, though it took some time for officials to understand what he wanted! Some say that he did succeed in hitting the hole but that the ball was going too quickly and raced through into the flower beds. Well, Hagen used to say that no one ever remembered who finished second and rather lost interest, taking four more shots to get down, yet still finishing third.

His appearances in the British Open now became spasmodic but he turned up again in 1928 and 1929 and won both. Just before the 1928 event at Royal St George's, Hagen suffered the biggest matchplay thrashing of his career when Archie Compston, playing superbly, beat him by 18 and 17 over 72 holes. It was unbelievable but some have said that once Walter had realized he was going to be beaten he thought that a really huge margin would make more headlines. All publicity was good publicity.

Archie Compston, perhaps the best British player at the time, was expected to win the Championship. Indeed he played well throughout, but only well enough to finish three strokes behind Walter Hagen. Hagen's bunker play was notably good that year and remember this was a few years before Gene Sarazen was credited with inventing the sand-wedge. Blessed with very strong nerves indeed, Hagen often played them like a chip shot, nipping the ball clean, with the knowledge of certain disaster if he erred in the slightest.

Sarazen was his closest pursuer that year but Hagen's last day was a great one: two rounds of 72 and level par for the last four holes, including the 15th, where he was in a cross bunker from the tee. The Prince of Wales (later the Duke of Windsor) presented the trophy.

Hagen's last British championship victory came in 1929, when he was in his late thirties. After the first round, he had given my father, Percy, the first man to break 70 at Muirfield with a 69, a six-stroke start. Hagen then proceeded to follow with what he thought the best round of his life, a 67 over Muirfield's 6,700 yards. It was particularly splendid if you consider he was playing with hickory shafts and a 'soft' ball. The course played far longer than it does today.

His start was shaky – bunkered at the 1st but there followed a flick from sand and he came very close to holing out. At the 2nd, he saved par with a long putt. Thereafter, he didn't falter. Hagen's round left my father trailing him by three strokes, but the leader with rounds of 71 and 69 was the great American eccentric, Leo Diegel. They used to call him 'three-round Diegel' because he always seemed to have one poor round in four. On the morning of the final day, that round was 82.

This wasn't quite as bad as it may sound because the weather was foul, with squally rain showers and a south-westerly gale. Hagen declared if any of the leading group could manage a pair of 75s that would be good enough. He did just that and no one else came close. He won by six strokes, helped by a driver he had brought along to keep the ball low in high winds. It had a bullet-shaped head, deep face and very little loft. After the championship, the 8th came to be known as 'Hagen's'. Measuring 455 yards and a dogleg, it was a tough proposition and had given Walter trouble earlier. However, he noticed that thick rough at the angle of the dogleg had been well trampled down by spectators. He deliberately played to it and went on to birdie the hole.

Hagen, occupied with exhibitions and world tours, didn't enter the championship for several years. His last hurrah came in 1933, when he was a few years past his best. For a while, he revived old memories with rounds of 68 and 72 to lead the field. Thereafter, he faded away and finished well down the field. It was the end of an era.

The British Open was Hagen's favourite championship. He used to say: 'If I can have that one, the others can have all the rest.' Yet Hagen won more of the four major professional championships than anyone except Jack Nicklaus. In the British and US Open his total was six. The US Masters came into being in 1934, which was after Walter's heyday. His score, as you'd expect, is nil. The US PGA, however, he dominated as no one else has before or since. The reason is that this major championship from 1916 to 1957 was decided by matchplay and in Walter Hagen there's little doubt that we have the greatest performer in man-to-man confrontation ever. The situation can arise in stroke play, after a tie. Here Hagen claimed: 'No one ever beat me in a play-off.' I daresay he was right.

Hagen played in the first PGA of all in 1916 and reached the semi-final. Partly as a result of the War, he didn't enter again until 1921, when he defeated the Cornishman, Jim Barnes, by 3 and 2. He didn't play the following year, the title going to Gene Sarazen. It went to Sarazen again the following year, this time with Hagen in the field. The pair met in the final, with Sarazen's victory not coming until the 38th hole.

The years which followed were all Hagen-dominated. Until the arrival of Tom Watson, Hagen was the only American to win four British Opens. In the PGA he became the only golfer to win a major championship in four consecutive years, 1924–27. Sometimes, of course, the matches were close but as Bernard Darwin once wrote: 'The difference between Hagen and other players is that he just wins and they just don't.' In 1925, for instance, it was the 39th hole before he despatched Al Watrous and he needed 40 holes to beat Leo Diegel. Later he won the final with some ease. Diegel was in his way again in 1926, this time in the final, but Walter again came through, this time by 5 and 3. The 1927 final was a great occasion, Hagen versus one of the famous Turnesa brothers, Joe. Turnesa took an early lead, with Hagen conceding some highly missable putts. Later he was to be more severe, even telling Turnesa that he'd got a tricky one and would he like some help in lining up? Gamesmanship? Certainly, but no one, Turnesa included, seemed to mind. They came to the final hole all square, with Turnesa down the middle and Hagen away off the fairway, apparently blocked out by trees. Walter made quite a performance of debating how he should play back to the fairway before hitting the green through a gap in the trees. Perhaps Turnesa was unnerved by this surprise for he dropped his approach into a bunker – and that was that.

In 1928, Hagen's reign came to an end in an early round, at the hands of Leo Diegel, who went on to win in both 1928 and 1929. The statistics of Hagen's performance over these years are amazing. I find it difficult to believe that any of the great names who followed him would have equalled them, had the championship remained matchplay. Between 1916 and 1928, he won 32 out of 34 matches and in his championship-winning years set up a run of 22 consecutive victories. In this event he also has another record – for sheer tenacity. He went 43 holes in 1932 before being beaten by Johnny Golden.

To the public and golf critics alike, however, Walter Hagen the man was even more interesting than his performances on the golf course, where his great strengths lay from within 80 yards of the flag. No one was the source of more stories than Walter Hagen and some were actually true. It was believed for instance, that Walter would often party all night and turn up on the 1st tee still in white tie, tails and dancing pumps and then play a round in par. Part of this almost certainly did happen (at least once) but the more prosaic truth is that he might turn up late, full of apologies, and then change into golf clothes. All this, of course, went hand-in-hand with his reputation of being able to drink anyone under the table.

Early in his career, Walter drank hardly at all but he was not in the least averse to cultivating his high-living image. Privately, however, Walter would point out that he could make a highball last longer than anyone else. After all, no one can be adept at the delicate chip shots and flicks from sand when suffering tremors of hand and arm! Perhaps he did drink more in later years and certainly said that the eventual collapse of his putting stroke was the result of a 'whisky jerk'. It's more likely, however, that Walter preferred not to admit that his phenomenal nerve was not immortal.

Despite his greatness as a golfer (surely we must rate him among the top half-dozen of all time), Walter saw the game as a means of enjoying the life style he wanted. As he said: 'I never wanted to be a millionaire. I just wanted to live like one.' It's been said of Sam Snead that he made a million and saved two; of Hagen that he also made a million – and spent two.

He was relaxed and fully at home with people from all levels of life – equally with those spectators he invited along to the pub for a drink and the rich and famous. Once, he kept President Harding, a keen golfer, waiting for quarter of an hour while he shaved (Hagen was, of course, late again). On another occasion, he showed that royalty didn't fill him with awe. Playing with the Prince of Wales (later the Duke of Windsor) he once said: 'Eddie, hold the flag while I putt this one will you?' Walter Hagen, among my Supremes, would certainly be my first choice for an evening's companion.

HAGEN, WALTER CHARLES
Born: Rochester, New York, USA, 21 December 1892. Died: 1969
Major championship victories: 1914 US Open Championship; 1919
US Open Championship; 1921 US PGA Championship; 1922 British
Open Championship; 1924 British Open Championship, US PGA
Championship; 1925 US PGA Championship; 1926 US PGA
Championship; 1927 US PGA Championship; 1928 British Open
Championship; 1929 British Open Championship.
Ryder Cup player: 1927, 1929, 1931, 1933, 1935
US Tour victories (1914–36): 27
Total career victories (1914–36): 54

GENE
SARAZEN

Largely self-taught, Gene Sarazen was a highly unorthodox golfer and a prime example of my precept that good golf can be played in some very unusual ways. From long-range, there was nothing unusual about him. His swing was neat, powerful, balanced and rhythmic. At close hand, however, his grip on the club amazed me. I don't think it could exist today. The first time even a high handicapper at the club caught sight of it, there would be words. If Sarazen had sought professional advice, I'm sure he'd have been told he couldn't hope even to be competent, let alone a champion, because of his grip. Yet Sarazen was a very good golfer indeed. The shortest of our Supremes, at 5 feet 5 inches, he got more out of a small frame than either his contemporaries or successors. In his peak years from the early 1920s to the mid-1930s only Jones, certainly, and Hagen, less obviously, were his superiors.

Sarazen had an interlocking grip (little finger of the right hand and forefinger of the left entwined) which was unusual though used by Jack Nicklaus and a few others today and popular enough at the time. So far, so good. The first unorthodox feature was that Sarazen had a very strong left-hand position, fully on top of the shaft. His right hand was less strong but even so, the V made by forefinger and thumb pointed just below the right shoulder. Today, many fine players have that V pointing at the chin or even slightly to the left of it. The most extreme oddity in the Sarazen grip, however, was the left thumb. Instead of tucking it into the palm of his right hand down the shaft, Sarazen had it more or less entirely off the shaft, touching the heel of the right hand.

Probably all this was the instinctive way Gene first held a golf club when he took up the game. In so doing, he almost certainly made the game more difficult for himself, as we shall see, but with much practice he made it work. Arguably, there are advantages. The left-hand position presents the side of the left wrist to the ball at the moment of impact, and is a position extolled by Max Faulkner, British Open Champion in 1951. It can give little if anything and, perhaps significantly, is the grip everyone uses when holding an axe. Collapse of the left wrist in the hitting area with the conventional grip is one of the most common and disastrous of all faults. Sarazen's method makes this unlikely, and a reflection of it can be seen among many players on the US Ladies' Tour. Women have weaker wrists and the strong left hand seems to be very worth while for them. Think, for instance, of Judy Rankin, such a good performer for many years.

What, then, were and are those disadvantages? The first is obvious enough. Any player with an orthodox swing who uses this grip will hook, pull hook and smother every shot away left, unless he compensates for the tendency to have a shut face at impact. Apart from not having an open stance, Sarazen was very like Trevino on the downswing. The hip movement and leg drive led all the way with hands coming into play very late. All well and good but, as we shall see, after great early success, Gene entered a fallow period, before rising to the top again.

He was born Eugene Saraceni in Harrison, New York, not long after
the turn of the century, very much a contemporary of Bobby Jones and
some ten years younger than Walter Hagen. The son of Federico and Adela
Saraceni, he grew up in conditions only a little above the poverty level.
His father was a carpenter with ideas above his station. He'd have liked
to have been a priest but that proved impossible. Although his education
was limited, Federico spoke polished Italian and his favourite reading was
the classics. Like many immigrants, however, he never managed to speak
more than stilted, heavily-accented English.

There was no real closeness between the young Eugene and Federico
and they grew even further apart over the years. Federico wanted his son
to follow him as a carpenter. Eugene had other ideas. At eight, he first
tried his hand at caddying, the route taken by so many of our early
Supremes. He used to give the money to his father. Golf introduced Sarazen
to a wider world and he soon had inklings that success at it could lead to
a better way of life. There were other jobs besides caddying. Like Hogan
later, he also sold papers and scavenged for scrap metal and coal from
heaps of ashes. In summer, he'd sometimes go fruit picking and there was
also a job which paid $3½ per week for lighting the street gas lamps.

In 1917 his father's small business was badly damaged when timber
prices rose sharply. Eugene had to leave school and for a while helped his
father on carpentry work. He had no flair for it, however, and was trusted
to do little more than hammer in nails. Increased opportunity to play golf
came as a result of illness. Eugene contracted pneumonia and was not
expected to live. The last rites were administered. However, he recovered
after a long struggle and for some time there was no opposition to his
playing golf: it was thought healthy for him to recuperate in the open air.

At about 17, he started his first real job in golf which was sweeping out
the pro's shop and cleaning clubs. He was paid $8 a week. In 1919 he
went to Florida to work in a railyard and also won some golf prize money.
This led to his being offered the job of assistant pro at Fort Wayne Country
Club in Indiana. His mother, Adela, wept tears of joy at his success.
Federico turned away without comment. No doubt he couldn't bring
himself to believe that this was any way to make a living.

In 1921 Eugene was appointed pro at the small town of Titusville, and
at the same time abandoned the name of 'Eugene Saraceni'. It was not
suitable, Sarazen felt, for a golfer – and was more suited to a violinist.
Shortly after, Gene Sarazen moved on to a larger club in Pittsburgh and
in 1922 he won the Southern Open. However, he was still an unknown
when he arrived at Skokie, Illinois, for the US Open that same year.

Sarazen began with rounds of 72 and 73, which put him three behind
the leaders. In the third round, Sarazen struggled to the turn in 40 but
managed to complete his round in 75, mainly the result of birdies on three
of the last five holes. He was still in touch, four behind the leaders, who
included Jones and Hagen. Such a gap can be closed very quickly.

In his final round, Gene reached the turn in 33 but then dropped a shot on the 10th. From there he parred his way in until the 18th hole which was a 485-yard par-5 playing into the wind. Sarazen got home with a couple of driver shots for a birdie and a round of 68, a very low score for the early 1920s.

He had been out early and set the target. Throughout the rest of the day, no one could quite match it and at the end he was the champion by a single stroke from John L. Black, a 43-year-old grandfather, and Bobby Jones, who had yet to win his first US Open. Sarazen was just 20 years old. Although he was not the youngest winner of the US Open, Sarazen did go on to set this record for the US PGA, which he won later that year.

In that same event in 1923 he met Walter Hagen, the greatest matchplayer of the day, in the final. Perhaps even more than in his US Open victory, Sarazen proved his worth in one of the greatest contests while this major championship remained a matchplay event. As Sarazen himself said of Hagen: 'There has never been a golfer who could out-think and outmanoeuvre a matchplay opponent as Walter Hagen could. You couldn't rattle Hagen whatever you did.'

Gene Sarazen posing for the camera in the late 1920s

It went to the 38th hole. Sarazen appeared to drive out-of-bounds but was in luck. He then sent his second shot just about dead to the hole and that was that. With this victory he had put himself very much on an equal footing with both Hagen and Jones as one of the Big Three of golf in the 1920s. In 1923, he followed Hagen's example and crossed the Atlantic, hoping to add the British Open to his record. He won a tournament at Royal Lytham and had the experience of playing 36 holes with Harry Vardon, who gave him the following advice about playing in strong wind: 'If I were you young man, I would never allow for the wind. You have a natural low trajectory to your shots. Always play right for the pin.'

It didn't work for Sarazen when he tried to qualify for the British Open at Troon that same year. After a first round of 75 he faced a rising wind on the second qualifying day. He took 85 and it wasn't good enough – many in the field had played in much quieter weather. Sarazen said he'd come back again even if he had to swim the Atlantic.

It was the beginning of a long pursuit and Sarazen did eventually win the title. He returned the following year and this time qualified but his rounds of 83, 75, 84 and 81 put him well down the field. By this time, Gene's golf game was decidedly off. During three years, he had won only one tournament of note. One reason was that he had begun to think about his swing. Gene later wrote: 'Perhaps the reason why it had all seemed so easy in 1922 was that I had no idea at the time how difficult the things I was accomplishing really were.'

He began to find that his low-drawn iron shots didn't hold the greens as well as he'd have liked. He thought that higher flight and a fade would work better. This meant cutting across the ball at impact and caused Sarazen to lose the groove of his in-to-out swing.

Of course, once he'd reached the top he realized that his grip was unusual, to say the least. He tried the standard Vardon overlapping grip. For him, it didn't work. He lost length on his drives and the punch went out of all his shots. The real problem was that he had come to the top as a young man, with a young man's ability to compensate instinctively for a swing or grip failing. It soon went and Sarazen slipped a rung or two down. It was to be a long time before he reached a peak again.

Although Sarazen went back to his original grip, he put in a great deal of time making it more secure. It wasn't until late 1931 that he felt he'd got it right. Before then, he had always developed blisters after prolonged practice, a sure sign the club was moving in his hands. This happened mainly because he 'lost' the club at the top of his backswing, letting the shaft slip down into the slot between right forefinger and thumb.

Sarazen had small hands, the main reason, perhaps, why he'd originally taken to the interlocking grip and he worked hard to develop the increased hand and finger strength he felt would put an end to his problems. He added weight to a driver until it was 30 ounces and made a point of swinging the club for an hour every day, both in and out of season.

Driving was indeed the main reason for Sarazen's decline. Early on, despite his tendency to hook, he knew he would miss fairways only on the left. He could aim down the right and give himself the whole width of the fairway as margin for error. Once his basic swing path became less reliable, he missed on either side.

However, from 1927 Sarazen began once again to win three or four tournaments a year but the prestige of more major championship victories eluded him, though he had a number of high placings in the US Open. He came close in the 1928 British Open at Royal St George's. Just a stroke behind the leader, 'Wild' Bill Mehlhorn, with an opening 71, he took 76 in the second round and could not score quite well enough in the final 36 holes to equal Walter Hagen. Later, Sarazen was to consider the 7 he took on the 14th – the Suez Canal hole – in his 76 the most damaging. He had been betrayed by impetuosity. His drive had found a doubtful lie but Sarazen had gone at it with a wood and fluffed his shot. Anger rising he had then gone at it again with the same club and found disaster. But perhaps this was the reverse side of one of Sarazen's great virtues, boldness. As Bobby Jones once said of him: 'The boldness of his play leaves him no middle ground. Gene just has to go for the flag.'

Sarazen holding his British and American Open cups in 1932

Like Hagen, Gene relished the challenge of links golf and was determined to put a final polish on his record by winning the British Open. He was eighth the following year and third in 1931 behind Tommy Armour, unlucky in having to cope with worse weather than the champion.

However, by this time Sarazen felt he had cured his grip problems and was a far more complete player than when he had first rushed into the limelight. By 1932, he had overcome one final problem, which was his bunker play. We are all used today to the high degree of expertise all tournament players seem to have with bunker shots but before the beginning of the 1930s it was a far more hazardous matter. The golfer had a choice of two kinds of shot. Using generally a thin-bladed niblick (about equivalent to a modern 8-iron), he could either flick it clean from the surface, a matter of great precision and nerve even when the ball was lying well, or play a strong blast shot – a matter of hit and hope. In this shot, the clubhead often cut too deeply into the sand, with the result that the ball died well short of the bunker lip. Equally, the head might skid through far too quickly, and take the ball clean. It would then whizz through the green into more trouble. All in all, a golfer had to be a far more skilful player to achieve fair to good results from sand than today.

The inventor of the sand wedge in action at the US Masters in 1984

Sarazen changed all that. He wanted a club where he could hit down behind the ball and for the head to ride through the sand and on to a good follow-through. Such a club didn't exist. Sarazen decided to invent one. Working in his Florida garage one winter, he fixed lead towards the rear flange of a lofted club. After much trial and adjustment, he produced the fore-runner of the modern sand-iron. Using this, he felt far more confident with his bunker shots and soon was reckoning to get down in two more from greenside bunkers more often than not.

At Prince's, Sandwich, he was favourite, for there was no Jones or Hagen. It was a very long course, almost 7,000 yards. Weather conditions were good and Sarazen was a long hitter. As Bernard Darwin wrote before the championship: 'He just tears the ball through the wind as if it did not exist.' Gene played both nines in 35 apiece, which gave him a one-stroke lead on Macdonald Smith, Charles Whitcombe and my father, Percy Alliss. On the second day he went one better, and led my father by three.

On the final day, Sarazen was one of the early starters and was out in 33, despite hitting a socket early on. This he made up for by eagling the 8th and having a birdie on the 9th. On the longer inward half he took 37, one under par. The round just about secured the championship for Sarazen. My father took 78 and was out of it. Only Arthur Havers, the 1923 Champion, bettered Sarazen's scoring with a round of 68. Nevertheless, he was five strokes behind.

Sarazen began his final round well, had a wobble or two but was revived by another eagle on the 8th. He coasted in with a 74 and a win by five strokes from Havers. His 283 beat the record 285 Bobby Jones had set at St Andrews in 1927 and was not beaten until 1950.

It was a sad year for my father. Although today the scores make it seem that Sarazen outclassed the field, my father used to tell me that this was still the championship he ought to have won. Although he finished nine strokes behind, what might have been, but for three-putting 23 times! Sarazen was to come into my father's golfing life a few years later, this time in the 1937 Ryder Cup. Sarazen called him 'a prodigious iron player' and indeed he was, though an unreliable putter. (During my playing career, people would come up to me and say: 'You're just like your father. He couldn't get them into a bucket either.') With nine holes to go, my father was three up but the American took three holes in a row and on the 33rd tee they were level. My father's second shot was just a few yards from the hole but Sarazen's careered through the green, his ball lodging in the lap of a woman's skirt. Not knowing quite what she should do, she made a decision that was fatal for my father. She sprang to her feet and the ball was lobbed onto the green. To add insult to injury his ball was inside my father's, who was stymied!

Although I have chosen Sarazen as one of my Supremes, I don't think my father would have agreed. He conceded that the American was a bold and good putter but thought his driving dreadful at times, plagued by a

Sarazen practising for the 1937 Ryder Cup watched by fellow team members (left to right): Sam Snead, Johnny Revolta and Horton Smith

quick hook, and he hadn't much admiration for his iron play, feeling Gene was not a very precise striker.

In triumph, Sarazen returned to the United States for the US Open at Fresh Meadow. There was no blistering start this time. His 74 and 76 left him way behind the lead. In fact, Sarazen was on such good form that he was trying above all not to make silly mistakes but caution wasn't natural to him. He continued in much the same vein for several holes of his third round until a sudden birdie, and the knowledge that he was slipping further behind, prompted him to go for everything. In this new mood, Sarazen picked up more than his fair share of birdies on the inward nine and his 70 pulled him up with the leaders. In the afternoon, Sarazen played some of his most inspired golf. His round of 66 gave him a three-stroke margin and set a US Open record for a champion's last round. Gene had played the last 28 holes in 100 strokes!

Undoubtedly, this was the high point of his career but Sarazen still had many achievements ahead of him. In the US Open, he was a close second in 1934 and produced his last performance of the highest quality in the 1940 championship, when nearing 40 years of age. Sarazen came to the last two holes, needing pars to tie with Lawson Little. With the aid of two good long putts, he got them. Exhausted, he sat down in the locker room afterwards and began to dictate: 'A ghost from the past came back to life today . . .' Next day, however, he lost the play-off with 73 to Little's 70.

Besides his national championships, Sarazen won two other majors. One of these was the 1933 PGA, his third victory in the event, one in which he holds the record for the most individual matches won with 51 as against Walter Hagen's 42 (though we should remember that Hagen entered only when he felt the mood take him after that astonishing sequence in the 1920s).

Sarazen's other major victory, and his final one, is one of the legends of golf. It came in the second year of the Augusta National Invitation Tournament, soon to be known as the Masters. The year was 1935. Sarazen began confidently with rounds of 68 and 71 but his third round 73 put him three strokes behind Craig Wood. For the final round, Sarazen was paired with Walter Hagen, who had the same score to that point, with Craig Wood out ahead of them. Hagen's chances quickly faded and he eventually finished well down the field with a 79. Sarazen himself wasn't playing particularly well but, like Gary Player, he always kept trying. Perhaps a miracle would come along. Well, one did.

While they had four holes still to play, Craig Wood had finished his round and preparations were afoot to make the presentations to him. No one had a chance of catching Wood, including Sarazen who would have had to birdie three of the last four holes. At the 15th he drove well, fully realizing he'd have to get one of his birdies here as it was a 485-yard par-5. For the second shot, the flag was to the rear of the green, an estimated 220 yards away. He took out his 4-wood, toed it in a little and 'rode into it with everything I had'. The ball carried over the water, pitched on the edge of the green and ran on, on and on and into the hole. It was a double eagle and Gene never tired of telling the tale at future Masters. He played out the remainder of his round in par, tied, and won the 36 hole play-off by 144 to 149. It was his seventh and last major championship.

It was to be many years before I first met Gene Sarazen. This happened when we were paired together in the 1952 Open Championship at Royal Lytham and St Anne's. On that occasion the casualness of his play put me off. Since then, I have met him many times and relish his charm, joviality and enthusiasm. If I must agree with my father, that he's not really quite of the same high standard as the others, Gene can still say: 'Look at the record books.'

SARACENI, EUGENE (GENE SARAZEN)
Born: Harrison, New York, USA, 27 February 1902
Major championship victories: 1922 US Open Championship, US PGA Championship; 1923 US PGA Championship; 1932 British Open Championship, US Open Championship; 1933 US PGA Championship; 1935 US Masters.
Ryder Cup player: 1927, 1929, 1931, 1933, 1935, 1937
US Tour victories (1922–41): 18
Total career victories: 36

BOBBY

JONES

Long, long ago, there was a time when amateur golfers could hope to compete on near level terms with professionals. Those amateurs were often gentlemen of leisure who could play as much golf as they cared to. Some played even more than professionals who also had to make clubs, give lessons, run a golf shop and, quite frequently, keep the course in good order as well.

Before the turn of the century, you will find the names of two amateur golfers who were British Open champions – John Ball and Harold Hilton. There were also others like Horace Hutchinson, Freddie Tait and Johnny Laidlay who were capable of winning it. One year amateurs were placed first and second and no one gave this happening as much as a single thought. But then the great trio of Vardon, Taylor and Braid established the dominance of the professional game once and for all. True, Harold Hilton came very close in 1912 as did Roger Wethered in 1921, but by then such amateur successes were the exception. The story is similar for the US Open, except for a brilliant period in amateur golf between 1913 and 1916 when Walter Hagen was the only professional to win.

What had happened, on both sides of the Atlantic, with rare exceptions, was that the man who played for money had outstripped his amateur counterpart. Amateurs with all the time in the world to play competitive golf perhaps lacked the very strong motivation of having to make a living from the game. One of the exceptions was Robert Tyre Jones Junior from Atlanta, Georgia. Now that Jones's dazzling achievements are more than half a century old, it's easy to forget that the man was an amateur. During his competitive career, which lasted from the age of 14 until he retired at 28, Jones was also occupied with gaining himself a good education at school, college and university and then having to earn a living. He played in the summer months only and even then played little sternly competitive golf, other than the US Open and the US Amateur Championships. He made just four trips to Britain to compete in the Open and Amateur Championships and Walker Cup. Otherwise, he entered only an occasional professional or amateur tournament to sharpen his competitive edge.

The most amazing aspect of Jones's career, whose greatest years were between 1923 and 1930, is that he played mainly friendly fourball golf, practised a little at the beginning of the season – then went off and won, say, the US Open.

Such a regime would be laughed at today, yet I suspect a Jones reborn could do it all again, just as Hogan, in his greatest years, almost totally restricted himself to attempts on the major championships. Hogan, however, practised intensively every day. Jones never had the time and almost certainly would rather have played a fourball with cronies even if he had.

With that kind of 'amateur' approach he made himself the greatest golfer of his day and was recognized in the United States as supreme among all the country's sportsmen. As Paul Gallico once wrote: 'Jones in his day was considered the champion of champions – in other words, better and more perfect at playing his game than any of the other champions were at theirs'.'

Bobby Jones was the second child of Robert Purmedus Jones and the former Clara Merrick Thomas. His parents had had an earlier son who had weighed a touch over five pounds at birth and had died three months later. Bobby Jones was much the same weight at birth and his chances of survival weren't any better. In the early years, his stomach rejected everything except an egg white and peas. What a diet! Doctors felt it remarkable he'd survived longer than his brother, and didn't think he would last much longer. Bobby was kept away from all contact with other people because they had germs that would kill him, as they had his brother.

In 1907 his parents took a house for the summer close to the Atlanta Athletic Club's East Lake course. His father and mother began to play golf. At much the same time, Bobby Jones did so as well, knocking a ball about near the house with a cut-down club. He was just five and a half.

The following year, his parents moved to East Lake permanently and let young Jones onto the course to knock a ball along behind them as they played. At this time, he had no tutor in the game other than watching the way his father and mother swung at the ball and perhaps the club's pro, Jimmy Maiden from Carnoustie in Scotland, who was succeeded a year or so later by his brother Stewart, who was to be a far greater influence on young Jones. He began to tag along behind Maiden and came to imitate the Scotsman's wristy upright swing. There were no lessons. Jones just worked it all out for himself.

At the age of nine, he won his club's junior championship. There were very few entrants but at least Jones was invariably breaking 100. By the age of 12, he was able to score in the 70s and was most impressed by an exhibition match in which Harry Vardon and Ted Ray were playing. He noted how Vardon had a smooth swing and seemed to par every hole. Ray impressed him far more, however. What a crack the man gave the ball!

At 13, Jones played in the Southern Amateur and reached the finals of the section for handicap players. At 14 he was club champion and playing in all the local events.

By now all sickliness was gone and he was of a strong, chunky build. The main features of his game were that he seemed to expect to hole every putt from 5 or 6 yards down and was able to pitch the ball near the hole from anywhere. That year Jones won the Georgia Amateur. His father decided to enter him for the US Amateur, on the face of it a surprising decision. He was still only 14, and Merion, still virtually unchanged in the 1980s, is one of the most testing of all golf courses.

Jones had to qualify for the matchplay stages. His first round, 74 over the easier West course, made him a certain qualifier, which even his 89 on the East didn't prevent. After the 74, the crowds gathered and Jones, unused to such attention, faltered. Even so, Jones qualified comfortably enough for the matchplay stages and got through his first round against Eben Byers, a former US Amateur champion by 3 and 2. In the next round Jones lost five of the first six holes to Frank Dyer yet still managed to trounce his opponent by 4 and 2.

He was a national sensation. Next, however, he met the reigning champion, Bob Gardner. Even so, Jones was one up at lunch. Towards the end of the first nine in the afternoon, however, Gardner produced a string of short pitch shots to save pars and the fight went out of Jones. They were holes he 'deserved' to have won. It was, indeed, to be many years before Jones became as good a player of matchplay golf as he was with card and pencil.

It's interesting to speculate how the 14-year-old prodigy would have fared over the next few years. By all accounts, though he couldn't control his temper when he played a bad shot, he already had a thoroughly mature golf game and might have won either the US Open or Amateur Championships. However, War came to the States in 1917, after Jones had won the Southern Amateur, and his competitive golf was limited to charity exhibition games.

Jones didn't play in the first post-war US Open but was second in the Canadian Open and reached the final of the US Amateur where he lost by 5 and 4 to Davy Herron, a man little older than himself. In 1920 he again won the Southern Amateur and made his first of only eleven entries in the US Open Championship, finishing in a tie for eighth place.

In 1921 his golfing education went a step further when he made his first Atlantic crossing with the visiting American team which beat Great Britain by nine matches to three. Jones won both his foursomes and singles comfortably in an event which foreshadowed American golfing dominance.

In the Royal Liverpool clubhouse at Hoylake there is a reminder of Bobby in the Amateur Championship which followed shortly after. It is what Jones called 'an old brass-headed putter' with which a Hoylake member, Allan Graham, trounced Jones by 6 and 5 in the fourth round. Worse was to follow. In the British Open, Bobby had the first of his encounters with St Andrews. He was to come to love the course above all others saying many years later: 'I could take out of my life everything except my experiences at St Andrews and I'd still have a rich, full life.' At the time, however, he felt dislike, mainly because of bunkering he considered illogical.

After two rounds of the championship Jones was on 151, a score that could have been a springboard to victory. On the final day, however, Jones's temper and game went to pieces. He took 46 for the first nine holes, dropped two more shots on the 10th and on the 11th, a par-3, was bunkered and took 5 to get his ball on the green. He pocketed the ball, tore up his card, cast it to the winds and stormed off.

Jones returned to the United States ashamed of himself and was heavily criticized. His temper had let him down again. However, it did not improve. Playing in the US Amateur, Jones thinned a pitch shot at the climax of a match. As he was apt to do after any bad shot, he flung a club. This one bounded along and hit a spectator, though doing no harm. Not long after, he received a letter from the United States Golf Association. It told him he would not be allowed to play in their events (which included both the US Open and the US Amateur, of course) unless he learned to control his temper. That temper is normal to all golfers. The better you are, the more infuriating it is to play a simple shot badly. In friendly play at East Lake he continued to throw clubs and swear aloud but in tournaments became utterly changed, a model that anyone could follow. Thereafter, no doubt the passions were as strong as before but they were kept to himself. Perhaps, like Sam Snead, he learned to be 'cool mad'. He never threw a club again in competition.

The US Open that year was dominated by the Cornishman Jim Barnes but Jones continued the learning process, moving up to fifth place. The following year he might have won but was foiled by a final round of 68 from a man about three weeks older than him, Gene Sarazen. Jones was second and reached the semi-final stages of the US Amateur. By this time he had a personal biographer, O. B. Keeler, an Atlanta journalist whose main brief was 'where Jones goeth so shalt thou also'. Keeler, looking back on Bobby's career decided that it neatly divided into two parts, the seven fat years of victory and the seven lean years of defeat. The truth of the matter is that Jones was learning how to compete and how to win in those lean years. He was a great player even younger, for example, than Seve Ballesteros and a major championship winner earlier, just a few months past his twenty-first birthday.

It happened in the US Open Championship of 1923 and his main adversary was a 5-feet 5-inch Scotsman from Grantown-on-Spey, Bobby Cruickshank, who had emigrated to the United States a couple of years before. At Inwood Country club in New York State Jones at last did what had been expected of him for years – but what a tortured business he made of it. Going into the final round he had a three-stroke lead and with three holes to play was level par. But Jones made it easier for his pursuers. On the 16th he put a shot out of bounds and dropped a stroke (the penalty then wasn't a stroke as well as distance). At the next he was through the green and took three more to get down. Worse followed. The 18th was a par-4 of about 420 yards, playing into a stiff breeze. This is how Jones played it: good drive; pulled fairway-wood; attempted short pitch over a bunker directly into it; and three more to get down. Bogey, bogey, double bogey. Four strokes thrown away in just three holes. There were those to console him who pointed out that he'd probably still be champion. Jones retorted, quite rightly: 'I didn't finish like a champion. I finished like a yellow dog.' Like Nicklaus 30 years later, Jones took great pride in his performance and hated making a fool of himself.

Behind him, Bobby Cruickshank didn't finish anything like a 'yellow dog'. He birdied the last to tie. Eventually, it seemed that he'd done Jones a favour. Bobby still didn't know whether or not he would crack under the pressure of the final stages of a championship.

The play-off with Cruickshank must have been reassuring. It veered to and fro with first the Scotsman in the lead and then Jones, who came to the 17th with a one-stroke lead. Could he hold on? No, Jones dropped a shot on the hole and they were level with the 18th again to be played dead into wind.

With the honour, Cruickshank pulled his drive and was obstructed by a tree for his second shot. He was bound to take three to reach the green. Perhaps with a more carefree mind, Bobby drove well and should have found a better lie than he did. It was sandy and he had to play a long-iron. The shot was not much under 200 yards with a water hazard to carry. In the same lie, I'm sure Hogan and Nicklaus would have been more 'sensible' than Jones and played short for a certain 5. Jones, a very quick player, went for the carry with a long-iron and struck a perfect shot to about 7 feet. Those so-called 'lean years' were over and he was the Open Champion of the United States.

Another well-judged pitch on its way from 'the master'

He was off on an unparalleled run in both the US and British Opens. In the American championship, he was eleventh in 1927. In his other six entries he won three, lost two play-offs and was second. In Britain, he won every time he played. For a spell of eight years in these two major championships Jones sustained a level of performance no one before or since has even approached. Two of my Supremes, Walter Hagen and Gene Sarazen, were also at their best in Jones's peak years but from 1923 onwards won neither of these championships if Bobby was competing. It used to be said that in every championship, and every one of the few events in which he played, it was 'Jones against the field'. That, I believe, applies to any assessment of Jones's position in golf history.

In 1924 Jones married. His parents had been proud of his early golf achievements and had encouraged him. His father was not a rich man but wealthy enough to foot some of the bills. His wife, however, resented Bobby's world fame and I suspect she might have been a factor in his decision to retire from competitive golf. If Trevino's new wife of 1983 told him there was life in the old dog yet and that he should go out and get those clubs winning, Mary Malone (Mrs Jones) had no such thoughts. She resented sharing him with the world and the absences from home his competitive golf involved. For her, that day in 1930 when he decided to retire was a particularly happy one.

In the year of his marriage, Jones won his first US Amateur. It's difficult to believe today, but for Jones amateur golf was just as important and matchplay even more difficult. Even though he was still only 22 in 1924, he had already been by far and away the best amateur for several years. But, as I learned to my personal cost, people often raise their game a notch or two when playing matchplay golf against a player they feel is their superior. Jones came to feel that impossible putts would be holed and chips that surely couldn't die by the holeside, down glassy-fast slopes, did so against him. Players who have earned no more than a footnote in golf history were apt to beat him. Jones might play well enough. Somebody else played the game of their life.

He decided to try and see matchplay as a hole-by-hole happening where he would try to par every hole, ignoring his opponent. For him, it worked. In his remaining years, a defeat for Jones became as rare as a Michaelmas daisy in a bluebell wood. In the 1924 US Amateur, he won his semi-final 11 and 10 and the final 9 and 8, both over 36 holes. Matches over 18 holes remained more of a lottery, but Bobby found that, for him, concentrating on par golf worked better than playing the man.

In the years 1924–30 he was champion five times, losing finalist once and in the other year, 1929, such are the quirks of golf, was knocked out in the first round.

About three months before Jones had won his first US Amateur, he had lost his US Open title. He finished second, beaten by an unknown Englishman from Hoylake, Cyril Walker. The following year, 1925, was not much different for him in the US Open. This time, another unknown, Willie MacFarlane, beat him. On the last hole, with Jones's round over, Willie had to get a long downhill putt dead over a frighteningly fast surface to tie. He did so.

Once again, Jones faced a club pro who had entered only because his home members had told him to give it a try.

In the play-off, however, that man in rimless spectacles, looking a touch like President Woodrow Wilson, stuck to his guns. It was his hour of unexpected glory. They tied with rounds of 75 and Jones then went into a four-stroke lead at 27 holes. MacFarlane then had three birdies on the homeward stretch and came through with a 72 to Jones's 73.

It was in this championship that excessive praise was heaped on Jones after he had called a penalty stroke on himself when his ball moved at address. Jones dismissed it impatiently saying: 'You might as well praise a man for not robbing a bank', such was his feeling that fair play should be automatic.

In the autumn, he made amends for the defeat by winning his second amateur championship against a fellow club member from East Lake, Watts Gunn, whom Jones had coached.

One of Jones's greatest years was 1926, but it started very badly indeed. There was a 72 challenge match in the spring with Walter Hagen, who never seemed able to cope with Bobby in strokeplay. This time it was a very different story. Jones played tidily enough but the difference mainly lay in the putting. Jones took about a dozen more than Hagen and lost by the margin of 12 and 11.

Jones took some lessons and then went off for his second visit to Britain. Five years had gone by. He was the number one in the Walker Cup team and his target was the Amateur Championship, to be played at Muirfield. He was one of the hottest favourites ever but was knocked out by a more or less unknown young Scotsman called Andrew Jamieson, mainly I suspect, because he was suffering from a stiff neck. Shortly after, however, he showed his mettle in the Walker Cup, trouncing Cyril Tolley, a name which will reappear in the Jones story, by 12 and 11.

The US Walker Cup team sailed away, leaving Jones behind. He had made a late decision to enter the Open Championship at Royal Lytham and St Anne's. First he had to qualify at Sunningdale and in doing so played one of the most famous rounds of golf of all. His first-round 66 had a sort of arithmetical perfection. He was out and back in 33 strokes apiece and hit all the greens except one par-3 in regulation figures (including being on all the par-5s in two). Through the green he played 33 strokes and took 33 putts. With the equipment of the day he almost always had to hit woods or long-irons into the greens, always the clubs where Jones had a clear supremacy over his contemporaries.

It was a different story at Lytham. Through the green, he wasn't at his best but his superb approach putting was at a peak. After the first round,

Hagen's 68 led by four strokes but a second 72 for Jones put him in a tie for the lead with 'Wild Bill' Mehlhorn. Hagen was a stroke behind and the Americans Al Watrous and George von Elm two and three strokes away respectively. These were the men who were to stay at the head of the field, with the exception of 'Wild Bill', who was to finish in 79 and 80.

On the final morning Jones took 73. It lost him no ground except to Watrous, who was round in the exceptional score of 69 to take a two-stroke lead into the afternoon's final 18 holes.

The championship was settled by a famous shot. With scores level on the 17th tee, Watrous drove well and put his iron shot on the green. Jones hooked from the tee into a sandy lie. He had to carry some rough ground and a bunker between him and the flag with about 180 yards to go.

Today, a plaque commemorates the success of the shot. Playing his mashie (about a 4-iron) into the wind, Jones carried the lot, leaving himself a medium-length putt. Watrous was unsettled enough to three-putt.

That clinched it, with Jones going a further stroke ahead at the last, after Watrous, like so many since, had found one of the many bunkers down the fairway.

Not long after, there was a ticker tape welcome home in New York and he then moved on to Scioto Country Club, Jack Nicklaus's future home course at Columbus, Ohio, for the US Open. Jones began with a 70, one of the best rounds of the day but followed it with a 79, which put him four behind the man who was to be his rival at the end of the championship, Joe Turnesa. On the final day, however, Jones began with a 71, to make up a stroke but was still four behind Turnesa with nine holes left to play.

Bobby was later to say that one of his lasting regrets was that he felt he had never taken a championship by the scruff of the neck and totally dominated a field. He was at his best when under the whip, as he showed over the final nine at Scioto. He parred the next two and birdied the 12th and on the next hole managed to get his par by running his ball through the sand and out to the holeside with his mashie. More pars followed with Turnesa faltering.

Even so, Jones needed to birdie the last, a par-5 a little under 500 yards. His drive was said to be more than 300 yards (a prodigious hit with hickory shafts and the balls of the day), and he sent his iron shot quite close and then two putted. He had become the first man to win both the US and British Opens in a single year. Since then, only Sarazen, Hogan, Trevino and Watson have repeated the feat. Even so, Jones comes out comfortably ahead, for he was to do it not just once, but twice.

At the end of the season, when Jones was also the beaten finalist in the US Amateur – losing to George von Elm, who had also featured in the Lytham Open – he began to dream impossible dreams. Could he do the Grand Slam, win the Amateur and Open Championships of both Britain and the United States in a single year? Yes, it sounds impossible today and, except for Nicklaus around 1960, there hasn't been an amateur since who could have seriously contemplated the idea.

Jones himself didn't rush into it. In 1927 he did defend his British Open title but wasn't an entrant in the Amateur Championship. He simply didn't have the time to play in both. At St Andrews he began by equalling the course record with a remarkable round of 68. It gave him a four-stroke lead. After a par round of 72 the second day, his lead was cut to two strokes but no one expected the man who had drawn close, Bert Hodson playing out of Newport, Monmouthshire, to keep it up under pressure and he didn't.

Jones followed up with a 73 and his closest pursuer was a very good golfer and teacher, Fred Robson. His 69 was the only other round under 70 in the championship from real contenders and one of only three in the entire event.

Jones's final round was a 72, finishing with a putt from the Valley of Sin on the 18th which just grazed the hole. He was the winner by six strokes and his totals of 285 beat the Open Championship record by six strokes. It was lower than any previous Open Championship four-round total at St Andrews by a massive eleven strokes.

This victory was perhaps his most perfect but for some strange reason it didn't go down into golfing legend. Why? Well, much of the Jones story centres on the near perfect iron shot or putt he made at a moment of crisis. At St Andrews, his victory was without such drama. He was expected to win, began by equalling the course record, was never threatened and made none of the silly mistakes that he often produced when coasting towards an obvious victory. Strange but true.

During the rest of his year, Jones failed to finish first or second in the US Open for the only time in the period 1922 to 1930 but, almost as a matter of course, picked up the US Amateur title, as he did again in 1928. It was all building up to the crescendo of his Grand Slam attempt – if he could manage to find the time. It seemed pre-ordained that 1930 would be the year. The Walker Cup was scheduled for Britain and Jones regarded the match as an unbreakable commitment.

In 1928 he had lost a play-off for the US Open and got himself into the same mess in 1929. For the first three rounds he was just about as dominant as at St Andrews. He began with a 69, the only round under 70 in the championship and his 75 and 71 which followed gave him a four-stroke lead into the final round. For the first seven holes, everything went well. On the 8th, however, racing his ball from bunker to bunker across the green, he took 7 on the par-4.

Ahead of him Al Espinosa was having troubles of his own. Playing the 12th already about four strokes behind Jones, he managed a triple bogey of his own and, as most of us would do, gave up any thoughts he might have had of winning the championship. He then had nothing but 4s and 3s and was leader in the clubhouse. But Jones still had five strokes in

Wet but happy: Jones after
winning the 1927 US
Amateur Championship

hand. Bobby now did his level best to give the Spanish-American the
championship, just like Arnold Palmer in the 1966 US Open. He dropped
a shot on the 13th but parred the next. At the 15th, however, a par-5, he
managed an 8 composed of a sliced drive, a misjudged approach shot and
a duffed chip.

At the next, he three-putted but then parred the 17th. He needed a par
on the last to tie. He got it with one of golf's legendary strokes. This time,
having played three, it was a putt from about a dozen feet, a downhiller
with a couple of feet of borrow. Jones got it in, a matter of precise
judgement and execution – with just a bit of luck as well. The next day,
he won the 36-hole play-off by 23 strokes. What a victory but, as Jones
knew better than anyone, it shouldn't have been necessary.

Now for the Grand Slam.

Jones had always believed that excessive preparation for a tournament
dulled the imagination, wearied the concentration and bored the brain.
For the 1930 campaign, however, he thought it might be worth while to
indulge in a little more winter play in the 'raw weather' of Atlanta, Georgia.
He also played a form of badminton to keep his weight in check, aware

that though a light eater during competitions he tended to make up for it at other times.

Perhaps, Jones felt, it would also be sensible to start competitive golf early. In doing so, he suffered his sole defeat that year. Playing a professional event in Savannah in March, Jones had a 67 and a 65 among his rounds but lost by one stroke to Horton Smith, a man who was carrying all before him at the time. Still in March, Jones played in the Southeastern Open. He made a sorry mess of the final three holes: 5, 5, 6. But despite such a weak finish Jones still won by 13 strokes!

In this period, Jones had learned something from Horton Smith. By no means a superb pitcher of the ball, he accepted Smith's counsel that part of the secret was to let the wrists cock further as the downswing begins. For Jones, and many others, it worked. He found that he was striking the ball with a new crispness and confidence.

And so to Britain for, first of all, the Walker Cup. Jones always took the event very seriously and was captain. The USA lost only two matches. The British Amateur Championship was next. Jones had played in it only twice but regarded it as the most formidable obstacle to his achieving the Grand Slam. So it was to prove. Over 18 holes, anything can happen. In the first round, Jones's start was brilliant in the extreme – four birdies in the first five holes, one actually an eagle when on the 4th at St Andrews he holed a bunker shot of well over 100 yards for an eagle 2.

Merely steady play thereafter brought him victory. There were eight more rounds to go, except the final which was 36 holes – but it was the 18-hole sprints Jones detested.

On the Wednesday afternoon of the championship week, he met an opponent he much respected, Cyril Tolley, a former amateur champion. It was blowing a gale and the greens were frighteningly fast. Jones went into the lead easily enough on the 1st, when Tolley topped his tee-shot but that was the end of easy pickings. The lead changed hands some half-a-dozen times and on the 17th, the Road hole, Jones had to sink an 8-foot putt to avoid going to the last one down. At the 18th, both drove to within a dozen yards of the green and Jones, a little too firm to be sure of getting through the Valley of Sin, ran 8 or 9 yards past the flag. Tolley, after a better shot, was left with a putt of a dozen feet for the match, but missed. They set out down the 1st once more. On this par-4, Jones was stone dead in 3 with Tolley stymied. It was all over. Jones had it when it counted. For the 18 holes, both had taken 75 in that brutal weather and it seemed as if the whole of St Andrews had followed the match.

Two rounds later, he met the American amateur champion, Jimmy Johnston and was sailing home four up with five to play. Jones then relaxed, and in the end had to hole an 8-foot putt on the last for a half to win by one.

In the seventh round, Jones had a fairly comfortable passage and on the Friday afternoon met the US Walker Cup player George Voigt in the

The classic Jones follow-through, poised beautifully on his left side

semi-finals. With five holes to play, Jones was two down but Voigt then obliged by slicing his tee-shot at the 14th over the wall out of bounds. He sliced again at the 16th so they were level playing the Road hole. Both followed what I think is the correct tactic by playing for the front of the green. Voigt's long approach putt was dead but Jones's chip was a few yards short. However, Jones had a comforting feeling as he stood over his putt: 'I could see the line as plainly as if it had been marked on the green. I knew I would surely hole that putt.' He did.

A par-4 on the last proved to be good enough and Jones was through to what he felt was the relatively safe haven of a final over 36 holes, even though his opponent was Roger Wethered, an amateur good enough to reach the play-off stage of the 1921 British Open. He had nearly withdrawn from it, thinking he ought to honour a promise to play in a village cricket match the following day! Such were the values of the times.

There was good golf for the first nine holes and they were all square. Jones then leapt ahead and was five up playing the Road hole. Here, he missed a 4-foot putt. As regards the match, it mattered very little but it put a 5 on his card and prevented Jones becoming the first man to play round St Andrews without a 5 or worse – something I accomplished myself many years later in 1960, when I had six 3s and twelve 4s.

As this championship was the one Bobby considered the most difficult to win, his Boswell, O. B. Keeler, wondered if his man would be able to key himself up for the British Open at Hoylake a couple of weeks later. But, as Jones later commented: 'To my knowledge I have never taken a golf tournament casually. It did not make sense to me to travel 3,000 miles for a lark.'

In the event, Jones's golf was not at quite the same high level as it had been at St Andrews – but it was good enough. He began with a 70 to share the lead with the young Henry Cotton and that old campaigner, Macdonald Smith. On the keen but very true Hoylake greens, his approach putting was deft of touch and left him with tap-ins again and again. On the second day, a 72 gave Jones the lead.

Jones felt that the first three holes at Hoylake presented no great difficulty though there are some who might disagree with this judgement as regards the first, with the out-of-bounds practice ground on the right threatening both the tee-shot and the following shot to the green.

On the final morning, however, he began 4, 5, 6 to Archie Compston's 4, 3, 4. The man who had been thought to have the measure of Walter Hagen at Sandwich a couple of years before was again adding a footnote to the history of the British Open.

Jones, after his morning's 74, set out on the final round knowing that Compston's 68 had given him a one-stroke lead. In the previous three rounds he had always started rather poorly but had managed the testing finish at Hoylake better than anyone. This time, he began more successfully and arrived on the 8th tee needing a couple of 4s to be out in 35 but he expected better than that, the 8th being a par-5 of considerably less than 500 yards, which was one of the clearest birdie opportunities on the course.

Jones drove well but just missed the green with his second shot. He was perhaps a dozen yards off the green with a mild upslope to chip up and the flag a further 5 yards away. Thinking that he mustn't be too firm, Jones left his chip just short of the putting surface and, still all too conscious that the green was fast, chipped too conservatively once more and left it about 3 yards short. The birdie opportunity was gone and he had to make this one for par. His putt shaved the hole and stopped a little more than a foot past. Crossly he went to tap it in – and missed. The hoped-for 4 had become a nightmare 7. He had used up five strokes from less than 20 yards when confronted by no problem whatsoever.

The rest of Jones's round was a battle. He played the next six holes in one over par and then faced another par-5 where a birdie was the target. The 16th was a long hole, 532 yards, but Jones knew he could reach it with wood, if he drove well. Jones made the distance but was bunkered in two at the left front of the green.

His ball lay well but the stance was poor, almost a one-legged shot with his right foot on the bank behind. To play it, Jones used a sand-iron which had been given to him by that very fine American professional, Horton Smith, some time before. He hadn't used it in earnest but it seemed to have just the right loft for the job. Jones almost holed it.

He went on to finish with a couple of 4s and felt that, despite his 75, the championship would probably be his. So it was to prove. Compston collapsed and in the end Leo Diegel had the best chance of catching Jones, perhaps even of winning. To tie he needed level par over the last three holes but on that same 16th hole took 6. Jones became the first man since John Ball in 1890 to win both the British Amateur and Open Championships in the same year. The impossible Slam was still on.

The next hurdle was at Interlachen near Minneapolis. On 2 July Jones arrived back in the USA to another New York ticker tape welcome. The US Open was just over a week away. The two British championships had been a tremendous struggle and had been played 'in the other man's country'. Although too modest a man to say so either before or since, and aware that the favourite can always fall at the first fence (as Jones had in the 1929 US Amateur Championship), he really felt that the US Open was by far and away the most difficult of the two tasks that remained.

He began with a round of 71, which put him a stroke off the lead, and followed with a 73 to be tied with Harry Cooper and Charlie Lacey, two behind Horton Smith. Jones liked the situation. He was not at his best entering the final day in the lead and felt that everything in his game was clicking into place, that ideal sensation when Jones felt that all he had to do was 'meet the ball'.

In the morning's third round, he went to the turn in 33 and after the 16th had added three more birdies. Years later, Jones was to feel that this spell of golf was the only time in his whole career that he had played his very best in a championship. Like the rest of us, the really low scores seem to come when we are swinging well, have the right feel in the fingers, good balance and rhythm.

Jones dropped a shot at each of the last two holes and had 'only' a 68. But he was five strokes in the lead, even so. In his final round, Jones had a 75, which included an absurd three 5s on par-3s. One of these came when Jones was coasting home, on the 262-yard 17th. At the last hole, Jones's second shot was on the green but there were about 20 yards still to go and two upslopes to judge. Three putts were likely and would probably lead to a play-off for the championship. Instead, Jones holed it to win by two strokes from Macdonald Smith.

This was the last time he competed in earnest against professionals. As we've seen he competed very seldom indeed in professional tournaments and in the Open Championships of Britain and the United States played in only 15, winning 7 of them, which was a near 50 per cent success rate that no other golfer has approached. Overall, that July day, he had completed a total of 51 tournaments of any kind and won 22 of them. It's difficult to believe.

Although Jones had made no decision on retirement, there was just one to go, the 1930 US Amateur. After winning the medal for the best score over the two qualifying rounds, Jones was not remotely pressed in the matchplay stages and wound up his competitive career with a 9 and 8 victory against Jess Sweetser, in the semi-final, before taking the championship with an 8 and 7 margin over Eugene Holmans.

We can speculate on the ifs and buts. Jones retired at the age of 28. One motive was that he wanted to capitalize on his golf fame but didn't wish to become a professional golfer. He capitalized in part by making a series of golf instructional films in Hollywood which were extremely successful and he also designed a set of irons that remained in production for more than 40 years. He also found competitive golf at the highest level almost unbearably stressful and, as I've already said, his wife was by no means a keen supporter.

Jones found playing championship golf a very great strain. After 1930, he was glad to be out of it. Anyway, there were no more worlds left for him to conquer. However, he did decide to reappear in 'his' tournament,

A rare family shot

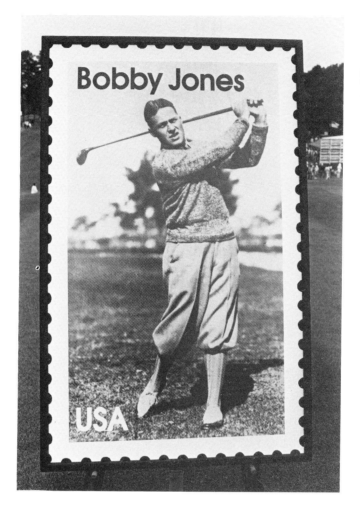

Very few golfers have been honoured by appearing on a national stamp and it indicates the respect in which Jones is still regarded

the US Masters, held for the first time in 1934. The crowds gathered to see that slow, full elegant swing again and their hero compete with the new generation. The swing was certainly still there but the man who 'always seems to be trying twice as hard as anyone else' no longer had his heart in it and, unused to competition, found his smooth almost floating putting stroke was gone.

In that first Masters tournament way back in 1934, he began with a round of 76 and, though he improved with a score of 74, followed by a pairs of 72s to finish, his total of 294 left him ten strokes adrift of the winner, Horton Smith. Even so, that thirteenth-place finish was Bobby Jones's best in the event.

However, he competed in the Masters mainly to lend the prestige of his name and had already long decided that, for him, competitive golf had ended that day in the autumn of 1930 when Eugene Holmans strode over to shake his hand and concede defeat in the US Amateur Championship final.

Jones's final years were as tragic as his golf career had been triumphant. After a couple of rounds in a Masters shortly after the Second World War he decided to withdraw because of a stiff neck. He told everyone he'd be back on the 1st tee the next year. It was not to be.

Jones was in the grip of a crippling disease called syringomyelia. That 1947 Masters was his last entry and, despite struggling to play in leg irons, he was out of friendly golf also some five years later. Progressively, he lost first the use of his legs and then arms. In his last years, a few thought it a little affected that he smoked his cigarettes in a holder. They could not know the reason. Jones's hands had become mere claws, almost without feeling. The holder was there to stop him burning himself. A very bleak end for a great star, perhaps the greatest of them all.

JONES, ROBERT TYRE (Junior)
Born: Atlanta, Georgia, USA, 17 March 1902. Died: 1971
Major championship victories: 1923 US Open Championship; 1924
US Amateur Championship; 1925 US Amateur Championship; 1926
British Open Championship, US Open Championship; 1927 British
Open Championship, US Amateur Championship; 1928 US
Amateur Championship; 1929 US Open Championship; 1930 British
Amateur Championship, British Open Championship, US Open
Championship, US Amateur Championship.
Walker Cup player: 1922, 1923, 1924, 1926, 1928, 1930

HENRY
COTTON

Sadly, I was never able to see Harry Vardon, J. H. Taylor or James Braid play competitive golf. This is one of the reasons I have omitted them from this book, great players though they undoubtedly were and all British (Vardon and Taylor were English and Braid Scottish). I believe Henry Cotton to be their only true successor though Tony Jacklin, with victories in both the US and the British Open Championships, runs very close. But I believe Jacklin's achievements, great though they were, are just a rung or two below Cotton's for the following reasons.

Cotton leads the major championship stakes with three victories to Jacklin's two; though Cotton's victories were all British Open Championships he has a better overall tournament record and his career at the top lasted much longer. Even so, Cotton's record is undeniably the weakest of our Supreme Champions. I've included no one else with fewer than four major championship successes and Cotton is also the least international of my choices. Cotton limited himself in his peak years to Britain and Europe. He did, it's true, make trips to the United States but not with the aim of putting the US Open Championship on his record-sheet; he went to learn and to build up his strength.

His first visit was at the end of the 1920s. Cotton hoped by gaining experience on the then broadening American tour that he could dominate European golf on his return. Nearly 20 years later at the end of the Second World War he set sail again, this time hoping to improve his poor health in a better climate and to get some good food under his belt, for rationing was still in force in post-war Britain. There were later visits when he played in the US Masters and the Open but these occurred when Henry was well into his forties and had little realistic chance of improving his record dramatically.

In explaining why he made no attempt on American major championships in the 1930s, Henry will point to the time consumed by trans-Atlantic travel at this period in his career. Even so, in the 1920s and 1930s, such American stars as Hagen, Sarazen, Jones, Leo Diegel, Craig Wood and Densmore Shute crossed over, sometimes with the sole aim of qualifying to play in the Open Championship, win it and depart on the next boat.

Cotton did not and so, as he says, failed to put 'an extra shine on my game and status'. However, in Europe he was far more active than his fellow British professionals. This was a time when tournaments were scheduled to end on Fridays. Golf club members expected their professional to be on hand at the weekend to dispense balls and tee pegs, give lessons and lots of free advice. But Cotton, even before he had an Open Championship to his name, was a cut above the rest. He was willing to risk his money competing abroad. Indeed, his first victory of consequence came in the 1930 Belgian Open, one of eleven continental open championships that he was to amass.

Some of Cotton's confidence came from his background which was very different from most club professionals'. The majority came into professional golf either because their father was already in the game as a professional (my own route) or as caddies, which is what my father did. Henry Cotton was born in 1907 at Holmes Chapel in Cheshire, the son of an iron foundry owner. In due course, the family moved to Dulwich in London and Henry went to a famous public school, Alleyn's. His first love was cricket but some conflict with school authority occurred so Henry gave up his bat and turned his full attention to golf. His brother Leslie was equally keen and both wished to turn professional which was just about unheard of for public schoolboys at the time who, whatever their sport, remained amateur though their sporting fame often proved useful when acquiring jobs.

George Cotton took his sons along for J. H. Taylor to look them over and give an opinion on their playing abilities when they were in their early teens. In his written report Taylor said that Henry would go the further for he was the more determined of the two and had better concentration. Significantly he didn't remark that Henry had great natural ability. Of course he had some but Henry Cotton, Supreme Champion, was the product of dedicated practice, ambition and the great determination which J. H. Taylor had rightly noted.

Cotton remembers that in the school holidays he and his brother would go off to their father's club, Dulwich and Sydenham, play 27 holes before lunch, the same again in the afternoon and then a final 18 in the evening! Academically, Cotton was potential university material but after matriculating at school gave up thoughts of reading civil engineering in favour of the life of a professional golfer. Yet Henry didn't see his future as a club professional. He wanted stardom. First came a long apprenticeship. It began in 1924 when Cotton turned professional and went as an assistant to the Fulwell Golf Club, spending most of his time sanding down the hickory shafts of the day and removing rust from iron heads. It was good for strengthening the hands but little more. Henry moved on to Rye, which offered more opportunity to play and stayed there as an assistant for a couple of years before moving as full professional to Langley Park in Kent. He had just had his nineteenth birthday but had seen and learned a lot.

Cotton now began to play a little tournament golf where he found that his long game seemed good enough but his short game wasn't. Throughout his career, Cotton was the worst putter of my Supremes and always seemed to make it look a rather uncomfortable business. The following year, 1927, Cotton made his first impression in an Open Championship. With opening rounds of 73 and 72 he was up among the contenders but Jones outclassed everyone that year. Cotton finished ninth which was a very good start. The next year he was eighteenth and was also runner-up in the *News of the World* Matchplay Championship. Already he was a promising player and determined to establish himself as the best British golfer.

He had been impressed by the American dominance of the British Open and wanted to find out how they did it. So Cotton arrived in the States in

November 1928 and stayed for about five months, playing the winter tournaments. In his first event he finished third but was also discouraged to find himself a much shorter hitter than most of the Americans. Like Bobby Locke at about the same stage in his career, Henry played with a fade. It gave him safe tee-shots which stayed on the fairway but there was some loss of length. Advised to try and draw his shots, Henry switched over to attacking the ball from an inside arc. His results deteriorated as he strove for more distance. Even so, he won prize money from time to time and returned to Langley Park with his life savings intact.

His long quest for the Open Championship then began in earnest. In 1929 he played part of the Muirfield Championship with Walter Hagen, who said he was 'a great hitter' but privately thought he had 'no polish'. Hagen advised him to come to the USA, believing that travel broadens perspectives. He felt the British should compete in the States and always urged his own compatriots that the British Open was a must. The following year at Hoylake, Cotton shared the headlines with Bobby Jones and Macdonald Smith as the first-round leaders but fell back to finish eighth, the sort of placing he achieved every year, his chances usually destroyed by one poor round. This was once more the case at St Andrews in 1933. He was by that time the club professional at Waterloo, Belgium, where the professional's retainer was much higher. He found also that his prestige was enhanced by the overseas base. Henry went into the final round with a winning chance. A whole cluster of players were within a stroke or two of each other. Cotton, alas, took 79 to finish seventh.

At Royal St George's in 1934 he had that self-same score in the last round but the outcome was very different. Cotton made a start which is still a record for the first two rounds of the championship, a 67 followed by a 65. Today it would be sensational; in 1934 such scoring defied belief. At the end of the first round, he led by three strokes but two of his most dangerous rivals, Gene Sarazen and Macdonald Smith were almost gone, with rounds of 75 and 77. Denny Shute, champion the previous year and another rising British player, Alf Padgham, were still there, however, both with rounds of 71. But the 65 put everyone to the sword. At the end of the day, he led his closest pursuer, Padgham, by nine strokes and the field by eleven.

What had happened to Henry's game? Strangely, in the light of his opening rounds, his form was very poor before play in the two qualifying rounds began. Henry took a break from golf two days before. Any further practice was just too depressing. He could hardly hit his hat. Then from nowhere, there came a 66, which was one of the best scoring rounds Cotton had ever played and he went into the first round proper in extremely good heart. He reached the turn in 31 and came back in par. The 65 was golf of much the same standard with a blistering finish of three 3s to make the difference. It gave birth to the Dunlop '65' golf ball and Henry was paid £150 a year for endorsing it.

Cotton at Carnoustie in 1931, his first Open Championship three years away

It has often been said that protecting a lead is more difficult than coming from behind. On the final morning, Cotton returned to the level of mortals. His 72 was by no means the best third round but it still increased his lead. His closest pursuers were respectively ten, eleven and twelve strokes behind. The congratulations poured in and the crowds gathered around the 1st tee to cheer home the first British winner since Arthur Havers in 1923.

Cotton, however, was well aware it was by no means all over. When he arrived at his appointed starting time he was told there would be some delay, due to difficulties in controlling the crowds. He went and sat alone in an empty tent. His mind was both full of the joys of imminent triumph and beset with thoughts of how comically appalling it would be if he threw it all away when a round of 80 would be good enough to win. The negative thoughts were seeping in.

Suddenly Cotton was seized by stomach cramp but the call came for him to take his place on the tee. Henry says that he could hardly stand upright but there is nothing in the rules of championship golf to allow anything more than the briefest of pauses. He had to go out and get on with it.

Easier said than done. Cotton was back to playing the kind of golf which had had him in despair before the championship began. His driving and iron play were no better than a medium-handicap golfer on a bad day. Henry reached the turn in 40 strokes and that first nine included three par-3s. It would have been even worse but for the fact that his putting was good. He started back with more 5s and heard that he needed an 83 to win. It was clear that Cotton wouldn't do it unless he could transform his game. On the 13th he at last got a good drive away and was nearly on the green with his second shot at this par-5. The chip was fair and he then holed a putt of 3 or 4 yards for his birdie.

The crisis was over. He reached all the remaining greens in regulation figures and all his approach putts died by the hole. Eventually, he took 79 and was champion by five strokes.

Although other British golfers were to win the championship in the years before the Second World War, it was Cotton who brought back the pride and was recognized as the premier player of the day. In certain limited ways he was the equivalent of Walter Hagen in being the first British player to make golf really pay. No one ever thought that Harry Vardon, James Braid and J. H. Taylor made a fortune out of golf. Cotton appeared to, even if it was a modest one by today's standards.

The man had style. His pro's shop, when he returned from Belgium to Ashridge in Hertfordshire, was the best in the country, spacious with everything set out in glass-fronted cabinets with seats and armchairs covered in zebra hide. He dressed well and loved fast and expensive cars, his favourite being a supercharged Mercedes-Benz cabriolet. Henry himself was also expensive, his fees for lessons and exhibition matches being far higher than those of any contemporary British professional. But he did not have Hagen's flair for public relations. His approach, however, was almost as effective, an aloofness, some said arrogance, that went well with his status as the 'maestro' of the game.

Indeed, it's remarkable how quickly Cotton earned this recognition. It certainly didn't come to Alf Perry or Alf Padgham, both winners of the Open in the following two years.

However, only Cotton among all British players since the First World War was champion a second time. The year was 1937 and the whole US Ryder Cup team was in the field including the new sensations, Sam Snead and Byron Nelson, and such relatively old timers as Gene Sarazen and Walter Hagen. Great Britain had expected to win the cup but lost by 7 matches to 3, only Cotton improving his reputation with a convincing 5 and 3 singles victory over Tony Manero, the 1936 US Open Champion.

In practice at Carnoustie they looked very good. They seemed, wrote Bernard Darwin of *The Times*, 'to do 72s like clockwork'. He picked

Henry looking happy at the end of the third round of the 1936 French Open, which was eventually won by Marcel Dallemagne

Snead as the most likely winner. In the championship itself, the 72s didn't come easy to anyone. After the first day the American Ed Dudley led the field with a round of 70 on the 7,200-yard course, with three British players – Bill Branch, Alf Padgham and Reg Whitcombe – a couple of strokes behind. Cotton took 74. On the second day, he improved to 72 but there was a new leader, Reg Whitcombe, with a total four better than Cotton's, who was by no means on his best form. His driving, chipping and putting were excellent but his iron play was off. He was missing many greens but saving par with precise chips and single putts.

For the last day's 36 holes, the weather was foul. It rained constantly, varying between heavy showers and deluges. In the morning, Cotton took 73 and made up ground on his closest rivals, drawing up to within three strokes of Reg Whitcombe. On the 1st tee in the afternoon he told a friend he felt he could win.

The last round, considering conditions which almost caused play to be suspended as greens became barely puttable, was one of the best of Henry's career. On the first six holes he hit only one green and birdied that hole. The others he negotiated with a chip and a putt – worth another birdie on the par-5 6th hole. He was out in 35 with the odds shortening on a Cotton victory. He made his way steadily home until he missed a short putt on the 15th. He knew he had to finish 3, 4, 5. It may not sound difficult, for that was one over par, but those last three holes at Carnoustie are perhaps the most difficult finish on any championship links course. The 16th is a par-3 of about 230 yards to a crowned green which usually has to be played with a wood and the 17th a long par-4 with the twists of the Barry burn coming into play. The 18th that year was not too difficult at 453 yards, though no one could relax with bunkers to the right and out of bounds all the way along the left and only a step or two from the green. Perhaps the true par would have been something like 3½, 4½ and 4½. Cotton got his par on the 16th and again at the 17th, needing a good putt to do so. A 6 would do it on the last and Henry didn't venture any heroics. He was content with par and a two-stroke victory. In foul weather, his 71 was only a shot over the course record.

It's surprising that Cotton didn't attempt to match himself against Americans on their home soil following his victory. Many rated him in those final years leading up to the Second World War as the finest golfer in the world. As Gene Sarazen later commented: 'I think he might have passed up a few of those Czechoslovak Opens in favour of visiting the States when he was at his peak.' Fair comment, perhaps, if a little sour.

After the War, during which his health had been poor, Cotton was in his late thirties and had lost a period of his playing career when surely he would have won at least one more championship. Had he another one left in him?

Ironically, Henry decided to go to the States again, lured by the weather, and food. He had always been extremely careful about his diet and perhaps that experience just before the final round at Sandwich in 1934 had increased his concern about it. He felt that good meat was a must – and that wasn't available in Britain with food rationing in force for several years after the War. Although it was improved health he was after, not a US Open Championship, he did win a tournament.

In Britain, Cotton was still the dominant player among the home professionals. The Australian Norman von Nida and Bobby Locke might be more likely winners whenever they teed up but no British player really threatened his supremacy. Cotton could have won the Open in both 1946 and 1947, though the champions in those years were Sam Snead and Fred Daly. Cotton moved into his forties, still winning his share of tournaments (his last victory coming in 1954 when he was 47). By the time the 1948 Open Championship came round, Henry felt his time was running out. He particularly wanted another title both for the added glory and the fact that another championship would enhance his value in the golf marketplaces.

After the first round at Muirfield, he was two strokes off the lead. The next day he went out and broke the course record with a superb 66, watched by King George VI. It gave him a lead of four strokes and one he was not likely to relinquish. Once he was in front, Cotton's nerve usually held up well. At one point in the third round Sam King caught him but Cotton produced a couple of birdies and still led by two strokes at the end of the day. That's certainly not a safe margin but his 72 in the afternoon was bettered by only two players, neither of whom were contenders.

Playing in the United States
in the early 1950s

If Cotton's decision not to compete in the States was rather odd, his decision after 1948 not to play in the Open Championship in the next few years was equally strange. He undoubtedly had the game to win again and showed this on his next appearance in 1952, when he finished fourth, outscoring everyone in the final day's two rounds.

To some extent, Cotton was concentrating his mind on activities outside competitive golf. He wrote books and articles in magazines, designed some splendid golf courses and became a much sought-after and expensive teacher. By this time, he was indeed a great authority on the golf swing and all the subtleties of the game. As Gene Sarazen, not a great admirer of Henry's, commented: 'There are few golfers who know as much as Cotton does about the dynamics of the golf swing and who strike the ball as correctly and compactly.'

As a theorist, he became the prime exponent of the dominant place he believed the hands should occupy in swinging the club and I could hardly

The hands are just coming in. Note the pigeon-toed stance

agree with him more. Others, however, tended to be even more influential and for a time their theories carried the day.

Cotton taught that a good golfer should be able to hit the ball well with either hand alone and, if the grip was secure enough, should be able to send ball after ball away without any grip adjustment. Finger strength was vital. He developed it himself in his youth by carrying a small firm ball in his pocket and constantly squeezing it. Later, as a teacher he was apt to urge his pupils to whack away at an old car tyre to improve hand, wrist and arm strength.

When others were preaching the gospel that the left side should dominate by leading the downswing to and through the ball, Cotton argued that there was no substitute for finding the back of the ball and whipping it through with the right hand.

Perhaps the truth lies halfway between. I believe that correct leg action is vital in maintaining a base for the swing but does not, as many have argued, contribute much to power. No one watching any very good player could doubt that the hands do most of it from a hundred yards or so into the flag. They are equally important in the long game but less visibly so to the onlooker while the actual player, with trained hands, may be more pre-occupied with thoughts of hip and shoulder turn and leg action.

As a player, there are some might-have-beens in Cotton's record which I think were the result of too narrowly conceived ambitions, but for me he is not only the greatest British player of the last sixty years but also the best ever.

After the early encouragement of his father, Cotton probably owed most to the drive of his wife, Toots, whom he met on his Argentine tour well over 50 years ago. When they met, she booked a long series of lessons, mainly, I suspect, with the aim of 'getting her man', and thereafter kept a very firm, even jealous, hold on him. A wealthy woman in her own right, marriage to Toots ended any financial worries Henry Cotton might have had quite early in his career and they always lived a life of great style, in Belgium, England, France and, for many years, at the Penina Golf Hotel in Portugal, which looks out over the course that Cotton transformed from a paddy field and is his masterpiece as a golf architect.

The name of Cotton will always be very much to the fore in the Alliss household because of his long association with my father, Percy, as they were more or less contemporaries in spite of my father being some 10 years older. Cotton was a man to be greatly admired for his tenacity and drive, and also for his encouragement of young players and his desire to show them the way. Many's the time I've heard him lecturing young assistants on the importance of manners, writing letters, little thank-you notes that mean so much, having clean fingernails and polished shoes: little things that perhaps a lot of people don't put much store by today but Cotton did and he certainly in his own way has been one of the most caring and most influential contributors to British golf, this century.

COTTON, THOMAS HENRY, MBE
Born: Holmes Chapel, Cheshire, England, 26 January 1907
Major championship victories: 1934 British Open Championship; 1937
British Open Championship; 1948 British Open Championship.
Ryder Cup player: 1929, 1937, 1947
European victories (1930–54): 30
Overseas victories: 2

BYRON
NELSON

In 1946 Byron Nelson lost in the quarter-finals of the US PGA Championships (which was then a matchplay event) and announced his retirement from tournament golf to a surprised world. Why he left the scene in his early thirties is still partly a mystery. He has commented that he tired of the lunches, speeches, cocktail parties and pestering that are all part and parcel of being a superstar. I've also heard it said that his wife was no Valerie Hogan. Valerie was content to follow Ben around the tournament trail while Byron's wife, Louise, was far more of a home lover. She didn't want to travel and disliked him being away from home. However, Bobby Locke has rather a different explanation saying: 'Nelson got into such a state before big games he could neither eat nor sleep.'

I daresay there's a good deal of truth in Bobby's comment. Certainly, when I played with Byron during the 1955 French Open Championship at La Boulie, perhaps only his third tournament appearance in Europe in his whole career, I thought Nelson's nerve dubious. Yet all the skills were still there, and he remained a superb striker and one of the very few players I've seen who attempted to hit every shot dead straight. Of course, you may be expecting me to go on to say that Byron was impressive but finished twentieth. Not so, and I was privileged to be there when the great man won his last tournament.

I noticed then a 'flaw' in his swing which was the dipping of his knees in the hitting area. It almost made me feel as if he ought to be hitting the turf a few inches behind the ball with every shot. Indeed a few years earlier, in 1950, Gene Sarazen had written much the same thing:

> 'Nelson's only mechanical flaw was that he played his arms very close to his body and was inclined to dip his knees as he came into the shot in order to facilitate his hitting action. At first this dip was all but unnoticeable, but it was the kind of error that was bound to grow larger. Before Byron went into semi-retirement in 1946, this dip was beginning to affect the firmness of his shot-making and today it is the chief reason why Byron has been so very unimpressive in his periodic attempts at a come-back.'

(I don't agree. I feel that Nelson made no real attempt at a return to full competitive golf. He just entered a tournament from time to time.)

Today, I feel that all Sarazen's comments about Nelson's technique, and my own 1955 opinion, were wrong. They were wrong because both Gene and I were brought up in days when there were different ideas about the 'perfect' golf swing. You see, Byron Nelson was a revolutionary swinger of the golf club and broke some of the rules that had long been regarded as Holy Writ. Sarazen's formative years came when the small ball, hickory shafts and the idea of hitting against a firm left side held sway. My own experiences were similar, except that steel shafts were introduced from 1930 onwards. In the States, the larger 1.68 ball became compulsory from 1931 but the 1.62 lingered on in Britain some 40 years longer. In this way,

Nelson during the great years of the early and mid-1940s

I'm a contemporary of Sarazen: both of us were brought up on the 1.62 ball.

Nelson was the first golfer to adapt fully to both the larger ball and the new steel shafts. With his technique, he couldn't have played nearly as well with hickory and the 1.62 ball, but it was a technique that came about as a result of as many hours of practice and experimentation as Ben Hogan, his exact contemporary, devoted to the problem.

Let's see now what some of the key elements in the Nelson swing were. He set up with the ball close to the body and in mid-stance, he moved the clubhead away from the ball in one piece. There was no early cock of the wrists; hands, arms and shoulders moved together, without a kink at all. At the top of the backswing, the hands were high and the shoulders had moved through 90 degrees or more but the hips had turned only about half that. The plane of his swing was very upright and the left arm remained straight, almost rigid, throughout.

As he started back to the ball, the wrists cocked fully and a strong leg drive followed this first movement. This drive continued through the hitting area with a lateral slide from hips to knees. There was no impression of a hit *against* the left side. On the contrary he seemed to hit *with* it.

All this sounds very much what you would see on most tournament practice grounds today, doesn't it? That's because some of Byron Nelson's 'keys' have become standard to most top players, namely the one-piece take-away, full shoulder turn, restricted hip movement, high hands and the downswing dominated by the left side. The reason is simple. He was the best player of the day, his techniques were widely imitated and they worked, for the best players. But what techniques of the hickory-shaft days had Nelson thrown out? The most basic change was that he shifted the emphasis from the hands to the lower body. Where most players had begun the backswing with a hand movement which 'left the clubhead behind', Nelson's was a one-piece action.

Hickory-shaft players opened the clubface as they took it back and gave a wristy flick at the ball trying to time hand action with the torsion of a hickory shaft. With steel shafts, Nelson didn't need to conquer these difficult techniques. Instead, he eliminated them. It was similar in the case of Jones's full hip turn. This went with the need to swing the club as fully and freely as possible, and to avoid a 'hit' at the ball. Steel shafts enabled a player to hit much harder and the restricted hip turn has led to a much tighter, more controlled action. High hands have helped to achieve greater length. Some features of the Nelson method haven't suited everyone. The rigidly-straight left arm, for example, has been used by only a few from Harry Vardon to Seve Ballesteros but both this and the unorthodox central ball position worked for Byron.

One way in which Nelson remained 'old-fashioned' was his so-called strong grip with both the Vs pointing a little below the right shoulder. For good players, this makes hooking almost inevitable. Nowadays, the left thumb goes more or less straight down the shaft and the right hand has moved a great deal more over the shaft: the Vs may even point to the chin or only a little to the right of it.

Even so, today both Lee Trevino and Bernhard Langer have strong grips in the Nelson mould. Why are all three not plagued by hooking? In Nelson's case, strong leg action leading the downswing was the answer so that the clubhead was pulled into the ball rather than flicked at it. Nelson's wrist cock as the first movement of the downswing was a great help here, enabling him to make the transition with the legs well in the lead. Lateral movement, with knees and hips sliding along the target line also helped.

However, as I stress elsewhere, how a player swings a club is only part, sometimes a rather small part, of a success story. Nelson retired at the age of 33 yet, as Sarazen says, come-back attempts, with what must have been the same swing as in his great days, were only partially successful. He won the 1951 Crosby against a very strong field, played well on his annual appearances in the Masters and there was that 1955 French Open win when he was 43.

To me, part of the story is that Byron had lost some nerve and the all-consuming desire to win. He was drained, like Bobby Locke after 1957, all passion spent and not the same man. Retirement with his wife Louise on a Texas ranch outside Fort Worth raising pedigree cattle had become a far more attractive life. You also quickly lose the habit of competing and, perhaps even more so, of contending. Of boxers, they've always said, 'They never come back'. In tennis, Bjorn Borg couldn't do it and in golf, as we see elsewhere, neither could Jones, when he began the Masters. Or you can take my own case. Totally out of competitive practice, and playing little golf of any kind, I've twice been persuaded to play in the Seniors' Championship. On both occasions I put myself on a diet, played as much as I had the time for but my main aim was far more not to make a fool of myself than to carry off the laurels. In 1982 at Longniddry I was really quite pleased to average about 76 per round and in 1985 at Pannal, the standard of my putting embarrassed me.

Nelson was not a great putter. They used to say when he was unbeatable that no one else would have bothered to enter at all if his putting had been of anything like the same level as the rest of his play. In one US Masters round, he hit every green in one or two strokes but only single putted twice – when he had tap-ins. That round brought him a 66 and I wonder what it might have been. Certainly at least three or four strokes below the Augusta course record of 64.

In his years of retirement, Nelson has been most helpful to those young players who interested him. Like me, he would probably never have been much use to a long-handicap player. But he helped two of the greatest amateurs of our time, Harvie Ward and Frank Stranahan and later the professionals Tony Lema, Ken Venturi and Bobby Nichols, all winners of major championships. Today, by far his most famous pupil is Tom Watson, who thus carries some of the Nelson trademarks towards the twenty-first century. Watson is particularly impressed by Nelson's play of the half-wedge shot. He tries to keep a mental picture of Nelson, hips and knees fluid through the ball, clubface square and on line for a foot either side of the ball and likes to feel his elbows and hips are following the same rhythm for every shot.

Nelson's reputation has suffered with the passage of time. This great player's record is often dismissed. 'They' say he didn't win enough major championships to be counted with the very greatest, and that his career was far too short a time at the top, most of his victories being confined to just a couple of years.

In a way, this is fair comment for I firmly believe that one test of greatness is the simple question: 'How long?' How long is long enough? Out of the same window could go Jones and Ben Hogan also; the peaks of their careers were only a little longer than Nelson's. The fact is that golf history has been a little too impressed by Byron Nelson's dominance from 1944 to 1946. It was so total that the remainder of his career has been relatively ignored. But he was no shooting star like Miller and Jacklin.

However, let's see what he did in that short space of time to earn himself the newspaper title of 'Mr Golf', which his implacable rival, Ben Hogan, didn't relish one little bit. Byron Nelson wasn't, as so many have said, a haemophiliac, but the comparative slowness of his blood to clot ruled him out of active service in the Second World War. After Pearl Harbour, there was little or no tournament golf but eventually tournament play was accepted with War Bonds as the prize money. At this point, Nelson became almost impossible to beat. In 1944 he won seven times and produced a stroke average of 69.67 for the 85 rounds he played, which was easily a record. 'All well and good', thought Nelson, 'but surely I ought to be able to shave a stroke a round off that next year?' Like Walter Hagen before him, but for different reasons, he'd kept a 'little Black Book', intended to record what had gone right and wrong in each of his rounds that year.

He came up with an answer. Apart from putting, which he'd decided he would just have to live with – good enough and no more – the answer was to strive to eliminate the silly shots. He didn't need to strike the good ones better or even produce more of them. If he could maintain concentration, that might do it. A stroke a round, from the evidence of the little Black Book, was within his compass. His greatest year followed. He saved not just a stroke a round but almost one and a half. At this time, no one else had previously managed to average less than 71.

One result was that Byron Nelson produced a sequence of eleven consecutive victories. On 11 March 1945, he won the Miami Fourball.

Yes, he did get into the rough, but not too often

And in bunkers

On 4 August the Canadian Open was his. No one, before or since, has bettered four wins in a row. Byron Nelson had 18 wins in all and an unofficial one. Some record. He won some $63,000. Today's level of prize money would have brought him in perhaps $2 million, about four times the sum anyone has achieved in one year. But even so there was a cloud on the horizon. In August 1945, Ben Hogan was discharged from the US Army Air Force. During the following year he more than challenged Nelson's dominance, winning thirteen times to Nelson's ten. The 'Mr Golf' contest was certainly on and there was much irony in this situation. Both had been brought up in Fort Worth, Texas; both had worked as young caddies at the same club. Their careers followed very different paths, Nelson achieving high status long before Hogan was even heard of. Indeed he'd retired before Hogan won his first major championship.

Yet, as regards the majors, Byron Nelson's record seems relatively weak, with 'only' five victories. However, this was in a period well before the idea of there being four such events each year had been established and the War took two or three of his best years.

On both sides of the water, the aim was to win the national Open and the respective PGA matchplay championship. Jones's tournament, the

Masters, attracted large crowds in its first year, 1934, as people wanted to see if Jones could still beat them all. When he didn't, the event slipped out of the limelight for a number of years.

However, as we see it today, Nelson's first championship was the Masters. In winning, he added lustre to the event. There was that perfect first round of 66 but he then fell behind that comet of the times, Ralph Guldahl, who entered the last round with a four-stroke lead. Nelson wiped that lead out at Amen Corner, playing the par-3 12th and the 13th, a par-5, in 2, 3 to Guldahl's 5, 6. He was to be a contender for many years after that. In 1941 he again came very close and was tied with the eventual winner, Craig Wood, after 63 holes. The next year, he tied with Hogan after four rounds.

He entered the 18-hole play-off which was then the order of the day with a distinct psychological disadvantage. After two rounds, he had led Hogan by eight strokes but his lead had leaked away. After five holes, he was three behind Hogan who played the next eleven in one under par. Little good it did him. After the 16th, Nelson was two in the lead and was not to be caught. He thought it the best spell of golf in his career. He

Nelson before the US Masters in the 1980s with his most famous pupil, Tom Watson

Prime Minister Harold Wilson presenting the Ryder Cup to Byron Nelson in 1965. On Nelson's right are Billy Casper and Arnold Palmer and on his left Dave Marr

continued to perform well in this event, even when long retired. As recently as 1965, when he was into his fifties, he opened with a round of 70 and finished in fifteenth place. This was into the age of Nicklaus. I think, however, that the US PGA was his best major championship arena. Between 1939 and 1945 he reached the matchplay final five times, winning in 1940 and 1945.

The US Open provided his fifth major championship victory and a controversial one it was. Snead took 8 on the last hole in 1939 and there was a play-off among Densmore Shute, Nelson and Craig Wood. After 18 holes, Wood and Nelson, with 68s, were still level with Shute eliminated. Out they went again, Nelson producing a decisive thrust when he holed a full 1-iron shot early on for an eagle and won with 70 to Wood's 73.

In 1946 he was involved in yet another 36-hole play-off, one that should never have happened. Byron's caddie trod on his ball and the penalty stroke might have made all the difference. The caddie wept; Byron Nelson put his arm around his shoulders and said: 'It's all right son. I was a caddie once myself. It could have happened to me.' After another 36 holes, Nelson this time lost but I think that gesture to the caddie says a great deal about the man. I have always found him, during our television work together, a man of great charm who, despite the pressures of his career, always had time for people. I expect that caddie agrees with me. For if it had been Hogan, then I think he'd have been more likely to have seen bared teeth or an icy stare, not a consoling arm!

NELSON, JOHN BYRON
Born: Forth Worth, Texas, USA, 4 February 1912
Major championship victories: 1937 US Masters; 1939 US Open Championship; 1940 US PGA Championship; 1942 US Masters; 1945 US PGA Championship.
Ryder Cup player: 1937, 1947
US Tour victories (1935–51): 54
Overseas victories (1955): 1
Total career victories (1930–55): 66
US Tour money winnings: $190,256

SAM

SNEAD

'Like classic plays and symphonies, Sam Snead doesn't just belong to a generation. His mark will be left on golf into eternity.' Such is the verdict of Peter Thomson who was thinking, of course, of perhaps the most natural, rhythmic and technically correct swing that golf has yet seen. Although I argue elsewhere that a great swing alone does not make a great golfer, it certainly helps! Here's another opinion, from Gene Sarazen who has seen them all from Vardon onwards: 'Snead is the greatest natural hitter of the ball since Jones, and perhaps the finest natural simple swinger of all time.' Snead certainly has a very natural simple attitude to the business of swinging a golf club, which is every bit as basic as Peter Thomson's: 'Ah jes' takes that club back nice and lazy and then ah try to whop it down on the barrelhead,' he once remarked.

Snead was born in May 1912 in Ashwood, which is a settlement of some 400 people in the foothills of West Virginia, some three miles from Hot Springs. He was the fifth son of Harry Snead, of Dutch-German extraction, and Laura, who was 47 at the time of his birth. Harry worked for a local hotel maintaining boilers and had a small chicken and cow farm which helped make ends meet for the large family during the years of the Depression. Snead grew up fairly wild, roaming the hills, trapping and shooting and trying to steer clear of all the moonshiners who were apt to shoot anything that moved on sight.

He first tried his hand at golf because his brother Homer, 12 years his senior, used to warm up his swing in the cow pasture. But Homer was no model for young Sam. His swing was rough and ready, though powerful, and he offered no help, either with the loan of clubs or advice. Sam's very first club consisted of an old head that he fixed to a whip and used to lash at stones. Next came something rather nearer a true golf club. Made of swamp maple, Sam used it to bat acorns. He measured progress by how many fence posts he could hit past. He learned early on not to slice. It was much muddier along the right and the rare luxury of a golf ball was hard to find. Perhaps slicing is the natural golf shot but Snead, experimenting all by himself with grip and stance, learned the 'natural' draw which has been with him ever since. Natural he may have looked, but like everyone else, Sam had to learn how to play.

At school he was an outstanding athlete but eventually decided to concentrate on golf for two reasons: he was injured at football and golf was an individual sport where he could rely on his own abilities and not be let down by the failings of others, as often happens in team games. Like so many professionals of his time, Snead was a caddie but was forced to give it all up when he suffered frost-bitten toes – shoes were for school and Sunday church-going.

He turned professional in 1934 in an unpaid job where he was allowed to keep any money he could pick up from giving lessons. Then he had a stroke of good luck. The golf manager at the Greenbrier Hotel in White Sulphur Springs saw young Snead hitting balls, was highly impressed and offered him an assistant's job at a living wage. At the Greenbrier, Snead was also able to develop his game and began to take part in competitive golf. In 1936 he won the West Virginia Closed Championship, one of his rounds being a 61, which was thought at the time to be a world record.

Snead matched himself against visiting professionals and decided that anything they could do he could do better. He determined to go to his first tournament to see what it was all about. The venue was Hershey in Pennsylvania. He didn't intend to play but, just in case, took along his set of clubs. There were by now nine of them, unmatched. They had cost him $9 and were worth not a penny more. Snead was invited to join in for a practice round. The start was embarrassing. From the 1st tee, he sent three balls out of play but put the next on the green, well over 300 yards away. Impatience and embarrassment on the tee changed to amazement. He scored well in the rest of the round and made up his mind to play in the tournament. No objections were raised, such was the informality of the

Awaiting the result of another superb shot

time. Snead finished fifth. He had proved something to himself. He decided to go out on Tour.

His next two events were not encouraging. To cover your expenses in the 1930s you had to finish very near the top virtually all the time. But at Oakland in California Samuel Jackson Snead struck gold. In the tournament, he tied with Johnny Revolta and Ralph Guldahl after rounds of 69, 65 and 69 and a final 67 brought him $1,200. Snead was in the headlines and was to remain there for some 40 or more years.

Snead made very good copy indeed. One reason for this was his driving. He was the longest hitter at the time and undoubtedly the first great player to regularly drive more than 270 yards. He was quickly nick-named 'Slammin' Sam' and, unfortunately in some ways, this was to stay with him for many years. That word 'slam' surely implies Snead was little more than a slugger. It tells nothing about the smooth wind-up and his balanced, rhythmical acceleration into the ball with no brute force in evidence. One writer refused to go along with the herd; he called him 'Swinging Sam' and stuck to it.

The other reason the Press took to him was the sheer romance that this hillbilly from the Back Creek Mountains, with no experience of the outside world whatsoever, should reach the top so quickly and apparently without effort. His hillbilly naivety was to produce a host of stories and the latest Sneadisms were always going the rounds. The very first came when a prominent golfer of the day, Henry Picard, showed Snead his picture in the *New York Times*, just after his Oakland win. 'How did they get that?' Snead asked, 'I've never been to New York in my life.' Fred Corcoran quickly saw the young man's possibilities and soon made himself his manager because: 'No Hollywood scriptwriter could have invented Sam Snead; he was the real article. He had the flavour and tang of authenticity, plus the magic promoters dream about, that extra quality that brings people to the ticket window waving their money.'

Soon after, Snead won the Bing Crosby tournament, but then went into a slump. The driving that had helped to make him famous was the main reason. Crowds turned out to see him hit the ball the proverbial mile and Sam felt obliged to try. He was not helped by the fact that tournament organizers always seemed to send him out with other long hitters, usually Jimmy Thomson or Lawson Little.

The fact was that though Snead was certainly a very long driver, he was also unreliable and especially when going for maximum length. Part of the problem was his driver. It was too light and the shaft too whippy. Henry Picard spotted the problem and gave him an Izett which was much stiffer and weighed about 14½ ounces. Snead loved the club as soon as he picked it up and stayed faithful to it for many years.

His form returned and, almost unbelievable for a player in his first year, he came to the 1937 US Open as favourite to win. He had competed in just seven tournaments.

His first round 69 gave Snead a share of the lead and following rounds of 73 and 70 left him one behind Ed Dudley and level with Ralph Guldahl, now a forgotten man but for a brief spell a marvel of the age. Sam's finish was the stuff that dreams are made of: a 3-wood on the last hole to a couple of yards or so and the eagle putt went down. Surely Snead had won. In the locker room both the Press and men with contracts for him to sign surged around. Snead was indeed champion – but only for a couple of hours. Out on the course, Ralph Guldahl had to par his way in to equal Snead's total of 283. Mainly by holing a long eagle putt, he did better and won by two strokes.

If Snead had won the championship that year, surely he would have gone on to win at least three or four more. At the time, it was a great disappointment but, they said, his time would come. It wasn't long after that Oakland Hills upset until Snead contended for his next US Open, at Spring Mill near Philadelphia in 1939. After two rounds Snead led the field with scores of 68 and 71. In the next round, Snead faltered a little, which included having one four-putt green. Even so, after a 73, he lay one stroke off the lead only. Snead went into the final round full of confidence. Those four putts were pure chance. His nerve was good on the greens. During this phase of his career Snead was a fine putter from all distances. With two holes to play, it looked as if he was going to break 70 which was probably good enough to win. As events later showed, a 69 would have given Snead a three-stroke margin and a tie with Guldahl's 1937 US Open record score of 281. On the 71st hole, he missed a short putt and bogeyed the hole but playing the last he still needed just a par to beat the best score in, Byron Nelson's 284.

Alas, Sam didn't know this and felt he'd have to try to birdie the 550-yard last hole. First, there was a long wait while the fairway was cleared. Snead then hooked his tee-shot into trampled rough. The lie was reasonable but there was still well over 260 yards to go, with bunkers to carry. The sensible shot was to play out short with a mid-iron, and then pitch on. But Snead believed he needed to birdie the hole and took out a fairway wood. The shot was not well hit and caught a fairway bunker, finding a slightly buried lie. With a 100 yards or more still to go, and a bunker face under his nose, Snead again rejected the safe shot, a sand-iron. Using an 8, he caught the ball thin and jammed it in the face. A few minutes later, Snead was left with a putt of a dozen yards or more for a 6 to tie Nelson. He took 3 for the most famous 8 in US Open history – at least until Tze Chung Chen's on the 5th in the final round at Oakland Hills in 1985.

In the space of three years, Snead had been caught by a very good last round to lose the championship and had thrown another to the winds. It didn't augur well for the future. Only once was he to come as close again. In 1940 he had a chance to win with a round to go but this time he really did collapse, his 81 put him well down the field. Another famous lapse came in 1947. On the 72nd hole, Snead holed a putt of several yards for a birdie to tie with Lew Worsham. It was neck and neck all the way in the 18-hole play-off and on the final hole both Sam and Worsham had putts of about 2½ feet to keep them level. Snead thought he was a touch further from the hole and settled down to putt. Worsham then raised a doubt and the distances were measured. Yes it *was* Snead's putt – and he missed and Worsham didn't.

The following year Sam trailed Hogan's first US Open victory by seven strokes but had begun with a pair of 69s and in 1949 was second, a stroke behind Cary Middlecoff. Sam's last real chance came in 1953, which was Hogan's greatest year. With a round to go, they were out on their own, Hogan having a one-stroke lead. Sam, however, could only finish in 76 (still good enough for another second place) to Hogan's 71.

Whatever he may say, Sam must have come to feel over the years that the US Open would never come his way. He'd thrown some away; others

Hillbilly Snead after winning
the British Open in 1946,
and hating every minute of it

had been snatched from him. How ironical then that he has a British Open title in his record. Why ironical? Because Snead just wasn't interested in playing it. He first played it in 1937 but was only entered because the whole US Ryder Cup team were in Britain. He hated Carnoustie and wasn't in the least eager to renew his brief acquaintance with linksland golf in Britain, this time in the first post-war Open Championship at St Andrews. However, he had contracts with Wilson Sporting Goods and the company's president insisted that he play. He said he would if Johnny Bulla went with him for company.

After a long train journey from London, Snead looked out of the window and beheld, 'some acreage that was so raggedy and beat-up that I was surprised to see what looked like a fairway among the weeds.' Snead turned to the other occupants of the train compartment: 'Say, that looks like an old abandoned golf course. What did they call it?' Yes, he'd arrived at St Andrews, which to Snead looked like 'the sort of real estate you couldn't give away'.

Snead's remarks did the rounds and he received a hostile press. He also didn't like the hotels or the food and he described the latter as an endless succession of baked beans, porridge and strong tea. But at least he knew the caddies would be all right, for hadn't he been told they were the world's best? Wrong. Snead later described his selection as 'a bunch of bums' who either whistled through their teeth or couldn't put the right clubs in his hand. His final choice was jailed for drunkenness the night before the championship began!

After the morning round on the final day, Snead, Johnny Bulla and Dai Rees led on 215 with Henry Cotton a stroke behind and Bobby Locke on 218. With the wind rising, so did the scores. Rees, for instance, went to the turn in 42, Bulla took three putts on each of the last two greens and Locke did much the same. Snead himself scored poorly to the turn. On the 6th, which he double-bogeyed, he hurled a club away in disgust and reached the turn in 40. However, he then birdied the 10th, 12th and 14th. That sudden move did it. He was streets ahead and coasted home to win by four strokes. From guess who? Bobby Locke and . . . Johnny Bulla.

First prize was the equivalent of $600 but it had cost Sam $1,000 in expenses to play. Always a man who took care over his small change, Snead decided then and there not to defend his title. Unlike Hogan, he did play again but only when years past his best, in the 1960s. He didn't value his win highly until much later, when this championship became the most important of the majors. At the time, Sam said it was 'just another tournament', and that his muscles and joints had ached for days from the icy winds.

The British Open was not Snead's first major title, though he did have to wait his turn before one came his way. In 1938 he had lost the final of the US PGA to Paul Runyan and again in 1940 to Byron Nelson. In the 1939 US Masters, he was second by a single stroke to Ralph Guldahl. His break-through came in 1942 when he reached the final of the US PGA and faced Jim Turnesa, who had beaten Ben Hogan and Byron Nelson to get there. Although Snead had won about 30 tournaments, the Press called him a 'choker' in major championships. However, Sam had had a premonition about this one and had delayed signing his papers for war-time naval service. His opponent was already in the army and had many supporters from his camp with him. Not only did they cheer Turnesa's every shot but also helped his ball back onto the fairway when Turnesa drove into woods.

After 23 holes had been played, Snead was three down – and felt nearly out. However, Snead didn't crack. At the end of the first nine in the afternoon he had drawn level and won the match by two and one when he holed a chip shot on the 35th.

Sam Snead had two more PGA victories, in 1949 and 1951, but in the Masters, after his near miss in 1939, he couldn't manage to come close for several years. In 1949, there were strong winds the first two days and Snead, with rounds of 73 and 75, was several strokes off the lead. In the last two rounds, however, nearly everything went well and he produced one of the best finishes ever in the Masters, two rounds of 67. In his last round he had eight birdies.

In 1952 the weather conditions were quite the reverse. The first two days saw perfect scoring conditions but were followed by what are said to be the strongest winds for two consecutive days ever at a Masters. Snead led with rounds of 70 and 67, but fell away somewhat in the third round. He had a 77 but few were doing better. In the final round, Sam was leading when he came to the dreaded short 12th, played over Rae's Creek, downfall of many a good man. The problem is that it's very difficult, from the tee, to judge what the wind is doing around the green. Snead's short-iron was dead on the flag but a flurry of wind knocked it down and it dropped short into the creek.

Sam angrily and carelessly dropped his ball into a muddy spot in long grass. From there he cleared the creek but only as far as the bank beyond. He took out his 8-iron, always Snead's favourite club, and ran it towards the hole. In its travels, his ball had picked up a lump of mud and it ran erratically over the putting surface. However, as it died away, the last lurch was a sideways one – into the hole. Snead went on to win by four strokes. It was a moment of good fortune to counter the ill-luck which had dogged him in the US Open.

His last Masters victory was the most memorable. When the four rounds were over he had come from three strokes behind Ben Hogan going into the last round to tie with him for the championship. Even so, not many gave Snead a chance in the 18-hole play-off. Hogan's reputation was at its absolute peak after winning three major championships the previous year.

After 12 holes, they were level and Snead went ahead when he carried the creek fronting the 13th green while Hogan played cautiously short.

Tortured by a putting twitch, Sam Snead found this odd method was the cure

That, plus a three-putt from Hogan on the 16th was enough. Hogan hit every green in regulation figures but his nerve on the short putts was beginning to go.

Putting had long been Sam Snead's greatest problem. Early on, he had modelled himself on Jones. Both stood to the ball with their feet close together and used a fairly wristy stroke. Some would argue that a putting stroke based on such hand action is the worst once the nerve begins to go. Snead's nerve went during a series of exhibition matches with Bobby Locke in South Africa in 1946–47. For a couple of years he found himself uncontrollably jabbing and jerking putts wide of the hole from as close as

12 inches. Snead tried everything including different putters, grips and methods. Even when he had finally made up his mind what type of putter he was after, he used dozens without success.

However, there was a happy ending. Snead opened his locker door at a tournament one day early in 1949 and found a brass centre-shaft model. He picked it up, liked the feel and used it at the Greensboro Open a little later. The long-awaited miracle had arrived. Sam's twitch departed and the putts started to drop. He won the tournament and was off on some of the most successful years of his career. Of course, I don't really believe it was the club that did all this for Snead. I suspect he just stroked two or three good putts with it and suddenly his confidence came flooding back – until 1960. The problem was not as bad as before for some years, but when leading the 1966 US PGA Championship, Snead produced a really severe jerk and hit his ball twice. In private, he'd been experimenting with a croquet style for putting. He straddled the ball with his legs and held the club with his left hand at the top of the grip and his right well down. It had worked for a few golfers who were either suffering from the same twitching curse or were just plain bad putters when using a conventional method.

Snead found that it certainly didn't make him into a good putter but he could make a passable stroke at the ball without twitching. I'm sure the pride of a Hogan or Nicklaus would have prevented them from using such a method in public. It does look rather silly. However, Sam decided it was either the croquet style or the end of his career. He was back in business with this method.

Unfortunately for Sam, the powers-that-be in the United States Golf Association and the R and A decided that it did indeed look undignified. So a rule was brought in to the effect that both feet must be on the same side of the ball when making a stroke. Snead countered by keeping the basics of his croquet style but positioning the ball to his right. All the advantage of being directly behind the ball and in an excellent position to sight directly along the line to the hole was lost but it did keep Sam working!

How Snead keeps going (and even into his seventies he can still play par golf as often as not) is one of golf's miracles. What are the reasons? Well, I believe they are both mental and physical. In the first place, Snead has retained his love of playing the game, both for fun and competitively. Of course, many high handicap players do too but I assure you it's much rarer among tournament professionals for whom golf is work, the equivalent of having to go to the office or factory. No one can play well much into middle age, let alone into their seventies, unless they play a lot of golf and enjoy it with a passion.

Physically, Sam was exceptionally well blessed, especially in being out-standingly supple and 'double jointed'. It may be no more than a party trick that he can kick an 8-feet high door with either foot planted flat on the floor but such a degree of flexibility means that he hasn't lost the ability to make a full backswing without straining years longer than would be possible for most of us.

All this has led to Sam Snead being far the greatest 'old' golfer ever. He was the oldest player, at almost 53, to win a US Tour event. At 60, he was joint fourth in a major championship, the US PGA, and that same year was in the top 50 money winners on the US Tour and he still competes on the US Seniors Tour occasionally.

The full Tour has in fact been the scene of Snead's greatest achievements for his record in major championships is certainly by no means as good

Swinging as well as ever: Snead during the 1972 Masters

as it should have been. But for his mental block, Sam would have won at least three or four US Opens and much the same in the British Open, if he had cared to cross the Atlantic.

There are no ifs and buts in his US Tour record, however. With 84 wins, he leads Jack Nicklaus by 14 and Ben Hogan by 22. Even as successful a player as Tom Watson is more than 50 wins behind. Snead is also an international golfer. He may have been unwilling to compete in the British Open, mainly because he liked neither the weather nor the prize money, but he is credited with 135 victories overall. Only Gary Player and Roberto de Vicenzo have compiled that sort of record.

SNEAD, SAMUEL JACKSON
Born: Ashwood, Hot Springs, Virginia, USA, 27 May 1912
Major championship victories: 1942 US PGA Championship; 1946 British Open Championship; 1949 US Masters, US PGA Championship; 1951 US PGA Championship; 1952 US Masters; 1954 US Masters.
Ryder Cup player: 1937, 1947, 1949, 1951, 1953, 1955, 1959
US Tour victories (1936–65): 84
Total career victories: 135
US Tour money winnings: $620,126

BEN
HOGAN

Here we have the most formidable of all our Supreme Champions. Even in the United States, where you are often on first-name terms even before you've been introduced, to the Press and public alike he was always 'Mr Hogan'. It's a small enough matter but it does tell us something about the character of William Benjamin Hogan, nicknamed 'The Hawk' in his own land and 'The Iceman' by the Scots, neither of which are exactly warm titles.

Fairly unapproachable during his playing career, nothing has changed much since. Hogan could, for example, have chosen to step into TV commentating, become a golf course architect, write about the game or be the world's greatest guru of the golf swing. What a procession of young hopefuls would have made a path to his front door to sit at his feet and hear the word.

Yet none of these things came about. He came, he saw and, after taking a long time trying, conquered. That was it. Always a very private person, whose calling required him to perform in public, he retreated into his personal life once again when his career as the greatest golfer of his day (and many think of all time) was over.

I have an illustration of my own. Gordon Menzies, a top Scottish television producer, was putting together a series on the development of golf throughout the world from the earliest times. When we reached the modern era, Gordon wanted me to interview as many of the great names as possible. All those included in this book who were still alive readily agreed – Nelson, Locke, Thomson, Nicklaus and so on. Sadly, there was just one exception, Ben Hogan. I had written him a formal letter inviting him to take part. His reply was polite and charming, but a firm refusal nonetheless. Speaking in front of cameras, he said, was just not the kind of thing he enjoyed. He hoped we'd all understand his reticence.

It seemed to me that he'd retired into his own private world where he enjoyed the company of only a few selected friends from Fort Worth in Texas and fellow members of the Shady Oaks golf club outside the town. I thought none the worse of him for you see Hogan had always been a loner. He didn't seek success over the long and bitter years because he relished the applause and fame. His ambitions were simply to be successful and, later, to accumulate a record number of major championships. He never came near fulfilling the second of these ambitions, great though his achievements were.

The adulation that was part and parcel of his successes just had to be tolerated. After all, he didn't seem to care much for people. Why did they appear to like him? He couldn't understand the reaction of ordinary people after his appalling road accident early in 1949. Why did they send him so many flowers and messages of goodwill? My great friend, the late Jimmy Demaret, used to say that this experience both humbled and mellowed Ben Hogan. He wondered what he had done to deserve all this affection. My own answer, and I think Hogan's too, is: very little.

For Hogan, golf was a kind of battle where he first had to conquer himself and then the course. Many have felt you ought to love – or at least respect – a course if you are to do well on it. To Hogan, however, it was the enemy, the son of a bitch that had prevented him from playing the 18 holes in 18 strokes. You may think I'm exaggerating but this is what Jimmy Demaret once related to me. Hogan told him that he'd just had a dream where he played 17 holes in one apiece but disaster came at the last, where he failed to hole out with his tee-shot and took two. He woke up in a bad temper. On another occasion, after Hogan had played a brilliant round of golf, scoring many birdies, he stalked off to the practice ground. A fellow tournament professional told Ben he ought to relax a little and said: 'Ben, you can't expect to birdie all the holes!' Hogan replied: 'Why not?'

He was born in 1912 in Dublin, Texas, the third child and second son of Clara and Chester Hogan; his father was a blacksmith and car mechanic. The first-born was christened 'Royal', the second 'Princess' and the third was definitely more fortunate with 'William Benjamin'. (Later, he re-arranged his initials to 'B.W.'.) In 1921, Chester Hogan found his trade in a slump and left his family for a short period to see if prospects were better in Fort Worth. The answer was 'just a little' and back he went to Dublin to give Clara the good news. She told him she wasn't prepared to move just yet, not until the end of the school term so that the children didn't miss any of their education. Chester thought this over for a while, went over to his suitcase, took out a revolver and shot himself in the head. He died a day later. At the time, Royal was thirteen years of age and Ben nine. Royal worked at three jobs to keep the family solvent and Ben sold newspapers. The suicide must have left scars, which were perhaps the more severe because there had been something verging on the ridiculous in Chester's death.

Already, much of Ben Hogan's attention was on golf. He caddied at the nearby Glen Garden club and used to knock golf balls along as he delivered his newspapers. He was a young fanatic like so many others have been. But we don't hear about the ones who gave it all up and went into another career. What Hogan most definitely didn't do was give up. For many years, he was the most persistent non-achiever of any of our Supremes and kept at it unblinkingly. He began playing as a cross-hander (left hand below the right for a right-hand player). This was almost certainly because Ben was a natural left-hander who started playing when suitable clubs were very hard to come by. Soon, he changed to a conventional right-hand grip.

By one of the odd chances of golf history he caddied with another boy who was later to be a fellow great player, Byron Nelson, and he also had a long wait for success. Their rivalry was to persist for many years; how vividly I remember Byron recounting tales of their boyhood duels to me. He was well ahead on points for many years but, despite Byron's remarkable pedigree, Hogan's greater persistence eventually won him more fame and a higher reputation.

Hogan turned professional at the age of 19 in 1931 and the next year set out for the California tournaments with $75 in his pocket. He had few successes behind him and reaching the final of the Fort Worth city championship at the age of 16 was the best of them. He didn't win many dollars and soon had to return home. The same thing happened the following year.

Hogan didn't have the reasonably secure base of being a club professional. He had to take odd jobs outside golf and then would blow all his earnings to play just a few tournaments. He was an oilfield worker, garage mechanic, bank teller, petrol pump salesman, waiter and even a croupier. My bet is that the last of these might have suited his personality the best. I can imagine that those cold as steel eyes beneath an eyeshade were easily able to keep the clientele in order and discourage thoughts of cheating. It was part of Hogan's desire to keep his privacy that he didn't like either his childhood problems or his years of trying to make good mentioned once the good times came along.

In 1934 he married the girl he'd known since both were twelve years old, Valerie Fox. She had many of the ideal qualities for a professional golfer's wife. She gave him unfailing support and was always happy to be his constant companion. Hogan loved her as she was understanding, strong and always utterly reliable. At tournaments she was there when he needed her but was otherwise content to remain in the background. Later he was to say: 'This is my trainer and partner. She takes care of everything. I have nothing to worry about except my golf game.' Despite the support of such a paragon, Hogan continued to be a loser. One problem was that he swung the club back much too far. At the top of his swing, the toe end came close to pointing at his left foot. This over-swinging may produce a little more length but leads to inconsistency, as Ben Crenshaw was to find many years later.

During this unsuccessful phase of his career, Hogan was indeed a very long hitter but some of this length came from the extra run his low, hooking flight gave him. As a result, he often missed fairways on the left, to find trouble in bunkers and rough. When he reached the greens, his putting was fairly poor. Hogan was never to become a superb putter but he did eventually learn a rigid, mechanical action that was effective from short range. His contemporaries came to think him excellent on the greens but this was only after he had become a great player. They were probably deceived into thinking that everything the man did must be perfection.

Before success came, Hogan always made his fair share of birdies but there were also likely to be several bogeys in a round. Bad shots lose tournaments far more than good ones win them. It took him a long time to cut out most of those poor shots and become a winner. Why Hogan persisted we shall never know, especially as the tour of those far-off days paid good money only to those who won or had consistently high placings. Total prize money was about $150,000 as against over $20 million today. Paul Runyan, leading money winner in 1934, took home just $6,767.

Hogan returned to the Tour in 1937 with no more success than before. At Oakland, he reached a new low. He and Valerie had just $5 between them, then he found that the wheels of his car had been stolen during the night. The tale is that this gave Hogan the determination of desperation. He finished the tournament in sixth place and won a life-saver, $380, which went quite a long way in those days. At much the same time, one of the leading players of the day, Henry Picard, offered help with money if Hogan needed it. He refused, but he had a life-line. Picard was also helpful in another way. He respected Hogan's game but felt that Hogan's shape of shot was his main problem. He urged him to learn to fade the ball. Well, the great majority of current tournament players think it's the only way to play. The drives land softly and that floating fade holds the greens. Today's players, helped by better equipment, hit further and can afford to sacrifice a little length when playing a fade.

In Hogan's case, length didn't come easily. He was only some 5 feet 8 inches tall and a lightweight, gaining length from great suppleness, a huge wide swing arc for a man of his size, wiry wrists and hands – and that low flight and draw. This is what Henry Longhurst wrote of him some years later:

> 'I watched Hogan closely in a practice round with Burke, Demaret and Claud Harmon. Each of these was driving a colossal sort of ball which, when it should have been descending, would bore onwards towards the hole, and it seemed impossible that a man the size of Hogan, who happened to be driving last, could reach them. Time and again, however, he lashed the ball along 30 feet from the ground, or "quail high" as they say in Texas. It ran perhaps 30 yards where theirs had stopped almost dead on the soft fairways, and finished 5 yards past the lot.'

So Hogan decided not to fade the ball. Instead, he began to control his draw better. The disastrous hooks became less frequent. At last he became a winner in 1938 at the home of the United States' favourite chocolate bar in the Hershey Fourball, partnered by the giant Vic Ghezzi. The following year, he took over as pro at the golf club there, where Henry Picard had once held the job and recommended him in preference to Sam Snead.

Life was beginning to look up for Hogan, now in his late twenties. In 1940, he 'arrived', first winning the North and South on Pinehurst Number 2 course and having four more victories that year. Soon he was leading money winner, a feat he repeated the following two years. With Snead and Nelson, he was suddenly part of a new triumvirate.

After Pearl Harbour, Hogan joined the US Army Air Force and left civilian life, still hitting the ball from right to left. When he returned, Nelson reigned supreme but Hogan was able to pick up where he'd left

Even Hogan was in trouble
sometimes

off. He won five times in 1945. It has been said that Byron Nelson's
18 victories that year wouldn't have been achieved if Hogan had been
competing throughout. This is unfair to Byron: all you can expect of a
golfer is that he beats everybody who turns up to play and Nelson's stroke
average was awesome. To adjust the balance, can I say I don't think Hogan
would have won quite so many events in 1946 if Nelson had not retired
that year. Hogan won 13 of them, a feat usually forgotten because of
Nelson's overwhelming record the year before. Only three players have
got into double figures on the US Tour. A table looks like this:

Nelson	18	1945
Hogan	13	1946
Hogan	11	1948
Snead	10	1950

Since that time the best results have been:

Palmer	8	1960
Miller	8	1974
Watson	6	1980

There was intense rivalry between Nelson and Hogan. They both came
from Fort Worth; both had been caddies at the same club; both had
struggled to make good. Nelson, while Hogan was away at War, earned

the newspaper title 'Mr Golf'. When Hogan won a tournament on his return, with Nelson in the field but 17 strokes behind, he remarked: 'Well, I guess that takes care of the "Mr Golf" business.' A touch of the green eye?

In later years, Nelson was slow to praise Hogan, unwilling to accord him the supremacy as a shot-maker which most others did. In fact the other great player of the trio, Sam Snead, once remarked that he couldn't bear to watch Hogan swing because: 'He took the club away so fast. It wasn't smooth at all, just effective.' Snead felt that his own much lazier rhythm would be badly affected if he watched and 'caught' Hogan's much faster action.

In 1942, Hogan had tied for a major championship, but lost the play-off to Byron Nelson. Ben won his first in 1946. This was the PGA, the event where Nelson announced his retirement after he had lost in the quarter-finals. After the first round of the final, Hogan was three down, but covered the first nine of the second round in 30 and went on to win by a decisive 6 and 4 over Ed 'Porky' Oliver. He was 34, according to his own record, though his friend Jimmy Demaret reckoned Hogan was born three years earlier than he would admit to, in 1909 and not 1912.

By now, Hogan had learned to fade the ball but was still prone to the occasional quick hook.

It was at about this time that Hogan devoted a few hundred thousand more practice shots (1,000 per five or six hours was roughly his rate) to ingraining his fade. He emerged in 1948 with what Cary Middlecoff, a leading player of the day, called: 'The worst banana ball slice you ever saw.' But Hogan was slicing them onto the fairway and slicing onto greens. He had more or less removed the hook from his game and his putting from about 8 feet in was nearly infallible. He won ten times that year, including his first US Open. A banana slice is just what no golfer wants, however, and in due course the basic Hogan shape became a lower ball which flew straight for most of the way and then tailed off right at the end. He had found his 'secret' and kept it very close to his chest. When questioned, Hogan said he hadn't even confided in his wife. (In 1955, however, he was induced to confide in *Life* magazine for a very substantial sum.)

With the tendency to hook under pressure, or when tired, gone, Hogan had reached a peak, particularly in the ability to score well when not on top form. At about this time, he had absolute trust in his swing. His dominance of the US Tour was only a notch less than Byron Nelson's had been a couple of years or so earlier.

In the first four events of the 1949 US Tour, Hogan won twice and lost a play-off to Jimmy Demaret in another. He decided to take a break. Driving home to Texas early one February morning in fog, his car was struck by a Greyhound bus which was travelling on the wrong side of the road. Hogan tried to protect his wife, flinging himself sideways. It saved his life. The steering wheel was forced through the back of the driver's seat but caught only Hogan's left shoulder, breaking his collar bone. The engine, however, smashed into his left leg and stomach.

Those first at the accident left him for dead and concentrated on Valerie, who proved to be not seriously injured. It was several hours before Hogan reached hospital where they found one leg crushed, his bladder severely bruised and broken ribs, pelvis, collar bone and ankle.

His obsession for golf still showed through, even in delirium. Convulsively, his hands made repeated motions of gripping and re-gripping a club and he called out 'Back on the left!' He was, of course, thinking of driving off with spectators lining the fairways, with the thought of hooking still troubling his inner mind! When he came round, Hogan immediately asked if he would be able to play golf again. The doctors very much doubted it but didn't say so.

Hogan healed quickly and after a couple of weeks he was thought well enough to convalesce at home. Then came a major setback, another operation to prevent blood clots causing a coronary. It was two more months before Hogan, shrunk to a skeleton, went home.

He still couldn't walk. In May he sent in his entry for the US Open, which was wildly optimistic. It was to be December before he played his first full round of golf – and that with the help of an electric cart. Soon after he managed a round on his own two feet. He immediately sent in his entry for the Los Angeles Open and when he arrived at the Riviera Country Club had still played only three rounds of golf. It was clearly foolhardy and perhaps idiotic, yet he almost won! Probably Hogan could not bear to wait to see if he could still hold his own – or more.

It was a new Hogan, still at the peak but playing far more within himself. Despite his terrible injuries, whose effects lasted the rest of his career, the swing was still lashing but a little shorter. He was no longer a full-time tournament player, his entries being few and far between. Instead he set his sights almost entirely on the major championships. Even there, he missed out the US PGA (still matchplay) because he did not believe his legs would take him 36 holes a day without intolerable cramps. As it was, he bandaged his legs up and soaked them in hot water after playing.

His most severe test lay just ahead and this was the 1950 US Open at Merion. The championship was then played over three days. Hogan would have to contend with a final day's 36 holes. Many didn't think he could do it, however well he was playing, and at least in that first comeback year, it's likely Hogan didn't know himself.

He began with rounds of 72 and 69, which put him two behind the leader, an old friend of mine, Dutch Harrison. After the morning of the final day, Hogan was still two behind a new leader, Lloyd Mangrum. Scoring was generally higher the final afternoon and, with seven holes left to play, the field had come back to Hogan. Two over par on the run-in would do it. But Hogan, too, faltered, dropping three shots. In

Hogan, after a tie with George Fazio (left) and Lloyd Mangrum (right) for the 1950 US Open, not long after his near fatal car crash

the end he had to par the very testing last hole, some 460 yards, to force his way into a play-off. He drove well and long-iron in hand, stood over his ball half a minute or more and then hit what Cary Middlecoff once called, 'the purest stroke you ever saw' and very much the equivalent of Tom Watson's 2-iron into the last green at Royal Birkdale to win the 1983 British Open.

So Hogan had survived the rigours of 36 holes in one day. Could he raise enough steam for the play-off with Lloyd Mangrum and George Fazio, who had both finished strongly? There was a chance that this could go to 36 holes also. But Hogan did it over 18, beating Mangrum by 4 strokes and Fazio by 6. The comeback from the jaws of death was complete.

Hogan now began to pile up major championship victories. In the rest of his career he won few events which were not in this category, so as not to sap his limited strength and going mainly for the glory and prestige of the major events.

In the next three seasons, he added his two Masters titles, two more US Opens, to equal the record of four, and played in the 1953 British Open at Carnoustie and, as the large crowds both hoped and expected, won it. He said he'd return, like General MacArthur, but never did.

At the end of 1953 he was on a peak that stands comparison with Jones's Grand Slam in 1930. In 1953 Hogan took three majors: the Masters and US and British Opens. No one had done that before or has

Ben Hogan in his greatest year, 1953, when he won the US Masters and the US and British Opens

repeated the feat since. He couldn't compete in the US PGA because the dates conflicted with Carnoustie in Britain.

Hogan had declared there was no reason why a man couldn't continue winning championships until 50, provided the desire remained high enough. At the end of 1953, with nine major championships won, his most certainly was. Would he equal Jones's total of thirteen? Would he set a target well-nigh unreachable for future players? Many thought so.

It's one of the peculiarities of golfing history that 1953 was virtually the end. He had several more chances and was twice runner-up in the US Open and Masters. One of these was unique. At Olympic Country Club, in 1955, the locker room crowd were congratulating Hogan on his record-breaking fifth US Open title. Out on the course, only an unknown called Jack Fleck had a bare statistical chance of forcing a tie – and only if everything came off for him.

Commentating on television, Gene Sarazen announced Hogan as the winner and the transmission closed down. Fleck had to finish one under par on holes measuring some 600 yards, over 460 and 337. In a trance, swaying and incapable of speech, he did just that. He came quite close to finishing with three straight birdies but eventually got the one that counted from about 8 feet on the last. Hogan stalked out of the locker room. I, for one, can't blame him. But, Fleck had been playing way above himself. Hogan would still win. Sarazen covered his pardonable error by saying he'd merely announced the result 24 hours too soon.

The next day, Fleck still inspired, was never behind. He led after the 5th, at one time increased his lead to three but Hogan fought back to be just one stroke behind when they got to the 18th tee. Hogan had the honour and hooked into very deep rough indeed. It took him three wedge shots to get onto the fairway, and that was that. Isn't it ironic that at the crisis his hook returned? Hogan, however, was not prevented from adding more major championships to his record by other people in trances. The truth of the matter is that his putting nerve was gone.

He had remorselessly drilled himself to force the ball at the hole from fairly close range, a method that worked less well when touch was required from longer range. By the mid-1950s, putting was a torment to him. The

Hogan shows that there's a hit in the golf swing — Cotton would have been proud of those hands

backswing got shorter, then almost non-existent. Sometimes, he would stand to the side of a green rehearsing all kinds of strokes, hoping to find one that gave him a feeling that it might succeed. Then he might stand paralysed over the ball for what seemed minutes. People wrote in to him by the hundred with cures. Knowing Hogan, I suspect he tried them all! His last victory came in 1959 when he won the Colonial Invitational and his final moments on centre stage were in 1967 at the US Masters, where he came back in 30 for a 66 at the age of 54. After this round, he was level with the eventual winner, Gay Brewer. On the final day, Brewer scored a 67, Hogan 77.

Arguably, Hogan is the greatest perfectionist and the most dedicated among my Supremes. It is difficult not to place him, at the least, as one of the three greatest ever. My one regret is that he was not a more giving man. The contributions he might have made to golf after his retirement have remained still-born and many of his golf secrets will go with him to his grave.

HOGAN, WILLIAM BENJAMIN
Born: Dublin, Texas, USA, 13 August 1912
Major championship victories: 1946 US PGA Championship; 1948
US Open Championship, US PGA Championship; 1950 US Open
Championship; 1951 US Masters, US Open Championship; 1953 US
Masters, US Open Championship, British Open Championship.
Ryder Cup player: 1947, 1951
US Tour victories (1938–59): 62
Overseas victories: 1
US Tour money winnings: $207,779

BOBBY
LOCKE

Elsewhere in this book, we see that great swings don't necessarily make great players. Several of my Supreme Champions have swings that, to say the least, were or are unorthodox. Bobby Locke's most certainly was as indeed was every aspect of his game.

In some ways, his swing was the exact reverse of Lee Trevino's who stands as if he were aiming 45 degrees left of his target while Locke used to aim just as far to the right, his right foot drawn back perhaps a couple of feet behind his left. He then took the club back well inside and reached the top with a very full shoulder turn, a fairly quick wrist break and more hip turn than is strictly 'modern'. At the top, the clubhead did not point down the target line but about 90 degrees right of it. From there he looped it back until everything was correct when he reached the ball. High-speed photography, however, does show that with Bobby there was little if any thrust of the right hand through the ball in Palmer or Hogan style. Instead, the dominant right hand was turning the clubface closed through the ball.

This meant the hook, feared by most good players, was Locke's basic shape of shot; a slow, looping flight starting well to the right and moving through about 45 degrees back to the fairway. Locke's hooking flight was not confined to the straighter-faced clubs. It's often been said that it's much more difficult to hook or slice with the pitching clubs yet a typical Locke approach was aimed down the right of the green and then drifted back to the flag, in a way which was fascinating to watch.

Even if you could keep the ball 'on a string' as Locke did at his best, this shape of shot makes it more difficult to hold greens, unless they are soft, because there is less backspin on the ball. Locke, however, didn't have a low hooking flight but a high one which always seemed to land softly. He appeared to get as much backspin as anyone else.

All this was a deliberate strategy. Locke had come over to Britain in the late 1930s while still an amateur. Although South Africa's best player, he had found himself being outdriven by most professionals of the day. At that time he was a very reliable driver but played with fade. On sun-baked South African courses he got enough length, but not in Britain.

The former Open Champion Ted Ray once advised, when asked by a pupil how to obtain more length: 'Hit it a bloody sight harder, mate.' But this sophisticated solution wasn't one Locke favoured. He had learned much of what he knew about the golf swing from a book by Bobby Jones which his father had given to him at about the age of 13. Perhaps he'd also seen some of the very popular Jones instructional films. Locke was impressed by the lazy rhythm and grace of the great American's swing and later felt he'd modelled his own on it. Although they looked very different, he always had a mental picture of Bobby Jones when he played. Merely hitting harder might destroy rhythm and balance. The solution he adopted was to try to draw the ball and therefore get more run on his tee-shots, without hitting harder.

Locke's strange position at
the top of the backswing:
who says the club should
point at the target?

One of his central beliefs was that there must be no tension at all in the golf swing. As a result, he gripped the club very lightly indeed. Although you may be able to *swing* a golf club with such a grip, it really isn't possible to strike a ball with much force and still retain full control.

There is an enormous degree of difference between top players in this matter of grip tension. Just by looking at the players, it's easy to see that, for example, Tom Watson is of the firm school and that Seve Ballesteros is not. Peter Thomson was of the same mind as Locke for part of the way but believed the grip tightened naturally in the hitting area, without the player being able to prevent it. Locke, however, thought he could do so and I see no reason to doubt him. So, equipped with that easy, light, rhythmical swing, Locke was soon on his way with the 20 or 30 extra yards that the draw gave him.

Locke's attitude to putting was similar. Here, one of his main aims was to strike the ball as gently as possible using a tender grip. He wanted the feeling of the putter almost falling from his fingers. Any tightness would lead to less touch on the greens. 'Hooking' came into his thoughts on putting as well. If he learned much about the full swing from Jones, it was Walter Hagen who was his putting mentor when they met in South Africa in 1936. Hagen advised that the club should be swung back with the blade hooded rather than allowed to open naturally. Locke himself later felt that he merely kept the putter face square to the line of his swing, as he took the club away very much on the inside, low around his right toe, which was drawn well back.

Some people declared that Bobby did in fact hook his putts into the hole and the player himself believed that his method imparted topspin. However, science has since shown that neither is possible. All putts leave the ground after they have been struck with backspin and if there is any slice or hook spin that disappears once the ball starts rolling towards the hole. However, even though Locke was, strictly speaking, wrong he did have a point. His method of striking put less backspin on the ball and one of the reasons his ball ran so far after so gentle a tap was the absence of slice spin. Locke was also most insistent that precise striking was essential. Watch people on the practice green at your own club. I'll wager you will see few who appear in the least concerned about how well they are striking

The best putter of them all, for my money. Locke at Wentworth during the 1956 Canada Cup (later World) Cup

their putts. Yet a mishit putt is one of the main reasons for the ball being short, though the player will often think: 'I didn't give that one enough'. Locke would sometimes give a demonstration of precise striking and its results. The perfectly-struck putt produced a light ringing sound from his steel blade. Others made a more muffled sound and the ball finished short of the hole.

What it all added up to is that Bobby Locke was just about the greatest putter who ever lived, though it's so very difficult to compare one generation with another. Nearly all today's tournament professionals seem to be very good indeed, as the game gets ever more competitive with a larger number of good players. Even so, in my 35 years or so as a competitor and commentator, I've never seen anyone superior. It's therefore odd to have to say that there were aspects of Locke's putting technique which few would want to copy. He appeared to have the ball 'too far' from his body and, more seriously, moved his shoulders a little from right to left as he came into the ball. The stroke itself was rather a jabbing one, with little or no follow-through.

If Locke was the best putter of his day, his short game on the whole was of the same level. Here, his feel for distance was superior even to Peter Thomson's. Locke might occasionally miss a green from, let's say, 150 yards but he was invariably pin high. His chipping was just an extension of his putting with the same feel and judgement for pace and distance. He carried three lofted wedges and always chipped with one of them, even when only a yard or two off the green with no obstacle between him and the flag. He never used a less lofted club or putter.

Locke came into golf very early at the age of four and was always encouraged to play by his father, Charles James. Both he and Locke's mother had emigrated from Northern Ireland to South Africa at around the turn of the century. There were two children, Bobby (grandly christened Arthur D'Arcy) and a sister three years older. It all, according to Locke, made for an 'ideally happy background'. His parents provided a calm unquarrelsome home, affection, loyalty and selflessness. In his father's case, he was willing to give up playing with friends in order to play with Bobby, no great matter, perhaps, but Bobby thought much of the gesture and how different from the lack of encouragement given to Gene Sarazen and Walter Hagen, for example.

In 1931 Locke won the South African Boys' Championship and a year or so later, at the age of 15, was down to scratch, and then plus 2. In 1935 he really arrived with victories in both the South African Amateur and Open Championships. The following year came that important meeting with Hagen on his world tour, who told him: 'Young man, your golf might stay still or you may become a great golfer, but remember that your golf education will not be complete until you have been to the States.'

These were fateful words but before that there was Britain, which Locke visited for the first time in 1936. In the Amateur Championship he was

The slim-line Bobby Locke of the late 1930s at Walton Heath

surprisingly knocked out in the second round but fared better in the Open, finishing eighth, seven strokes behind Alf Padgham. In 1937 he was again dismissed early from the Amateur and in the Open was up with the leaders after two rounds but fell away in the bad weather of the final day, having much the same experience the following year, by which time he was a professional. Because of the rules of the day, he was allowed to compete in very few events until he had served his apprenticeship. One of these was the Irish Open which he won, his first success outside South Africa.

In the last Open Championship before the Second World War, Locke had a remarkable first round at St Andrews. Coming off the 13th green, he was six-under-level fours but then met trouble in Hell bunker on the 14th and took 8. Even so, he was round in 70 to tie for the lead. The next day, the 14th was again unkind. Locke's hook didn't take on his tee-shot and he went out of bounds over the wall. However, he remained in contention. But what a costly hole.

In the War, Locke was a pilot, flying Liberators and did not play golf for two and a half years. After the War, a new Locke emerged. The slim 6-footer had now filled out and weighed over 14 stones. Eager to compete once more, he spent seven days on the journey by Avro Anson to Britain and was quickly a big name. He won three events and finished joint runner-up in the Open Championship behind Sam Snead, whom he invited to South Africa for a series of matches.

Snead, then rated just about the best golfer in the world, with Byron

Nelson retired and Ben Hogan not quite at his peak, agreed to the matches. Locke won the series by the huge margin of 12 to 2. It convinced him that he ought to go to the States. Snead himself felt he had been totally outputted. He wrote: 'What discouraged me was the way old "Droopy Jowls" held his putter at the very tip and with his left hand far over the shaft, which was the same grip he used on all shots. The standard reverse overlap grip wasn't for Locke. He had a closed stance and hooked his putts. His grip was so light I thought he'd drop the stick. And when he putted, instead of keeping still, he swayed like a Bloomer girl!'

Snead reckoned his shots to the green were inside Locke's three-quarters of the time but he still lost. Locke asked Snead: 'D'you think I could come to the States and make a bean or two?' 'You could get rich,' replied Snead who was so unnerved by the experience that he developed a twitch on the greens for a couple of years. So Locke decided to try his luck in the States.

His first appearance was in the Masters where someone said: 'The old guy (Locke was still only 30!) has the worst swing ever. Look at those floppy wrists.' He finished fourteenth but then produced this sequence: first, first, third, first. The last victory caused a great stir. Hogan had led him by five after two rounds but Locke got home with four strokes to spare. This 'guy from the jungle', Americans decided, must have something.

That first season he produced easily the best record ever achieved by an overseas golfer. Indeed, it still is. He won seven events and was just behind Jimmy Demaret, who played the whole year, as leading money winner. He also won the unofficial Tam O' Shanter event, being paid the unheard-of sum of $5,000 to compete and then winning it and the first prize of $7,000, far more than was available for any other tournament or championship. Locke returned to the States the following year and was again successful, taking three events and doing well in many others. One of his wins was in the Chicago Victory Open where his margin of 16 strokes set a US Tour record which still stands today. By this time, some American players resented both his success and the sometimes high appearance money he collected. He was banned from playing the Tour by the US PGA on the pretext that he had failed to turn up for two events for which he had been entered. Other Americans considered this ban disgraceful and though it was lifted fairly soon it left a sour taste in the South African's mouth. Thereafter, he competed less frequently. He had, anyway, thoroughly proved himself in the States and was happier competing in Britain and Europe.

His target was the British Open, and when Locke returned to Britain in 1949, he was immediately the favourite for the event, held that year at Royal St George's. He was already a success in Britain and his feats in the United States had very much enhanced his prestige. Anyone who could beat Locke would be champion. The event went much according to the script, though Locke didn't have it all his own way. He might have led after the first round but sliced a drive out of bounds towards the end of his round and eventually came in with a 69, two off the lead.

In stiff winds on the second day, he fell further behind as also did Harry Bradshaw who was on peak form and putting with total confidence. It was in this round, however, that the famous 'broken bottle' incident occurred. At the 5th, Harry found his ball resting against broken glass. Golfers seldom asked for a ruling from officials those days and Harry gave ball and glass a whack. However, when I spoke to him at Portmarnock in the spring of 1985, he told me that it had unsettled him and his putting was off for the rest of his round.

Both Locke and the Irishman were at their best on the morning of the final day, each round in 68s to catch the field. In the afternoon, Locke went out in 32 but faltered on the way back. He had to par the last three holes in 3, 4, 4 to tie Bradshaw. He did it the hard way, with 4, 3, 4. In the play-off over 36 holes, Locke was coldly determined to 'kill' the friendly Irishman and a ruthless job he made of it. First, however, he demanded that the hole positions be changed. To us today it must seem ludicrous – they had not been moved for the four rounds of the championship and the area round the holes must have been very worn indeed.

Locke's 67 to Bradshaw's 74 made the afternoon round almost a formality. Locke didn't have a 5 on his card in either round until the 33rd hole and won by a street – twelve strokes. It was all done with much the same philosophy that Peter Thomson adopted later: get the tee-shot on the fairway and long enough to reach the green in two. Thereafter, they differed a little. Locke then aimed to single putt. He seldom had a bad day on the greens. A poor putting round for Locke would have been a good one for almost anyone else. I consider him the best long- and medium-length putter I've ever seen, his ball rolling on and on, oh so slowly, to finish stone dead or in.

His putter did its stuff at the next British Open at Troon and his accurate driving with a 2-wood avoided the tenacious rough. During the second round there was dramatic evidence of Bobby's ability to put a bad shot or hole behind him. He said: 'I just blame the human element and leave it at that, after all, I may hit a few exceptionally good ones later. If you give it a chance, things balance out in the end.'

The 5th would have killed off many players. On this par-3, Locke was well short with his tee-shot and in long grass. He followed that by pitching into a bunker, taking two to get out – a triple bogey 6 resulted. Shortly after, he was again in trouble on a par-3, the Postage Stamp. Bunkered twice, he escaped with a 4. How often I've seen Locke play quite a lot of poor golf but still come in with a 72, as he did on this occasion.

On the final day, he compiled rounds of 70 and 68 to win by two strokes from Roberto de Vicenzo with Dai Rees and Fred Daly joint third. At the end of it all, Locke went for a drink immediately. He said he would have collapsed otherwise. Even so, the man always seemed unperturbable.

Looking at Bobby marching in stately fashion up the fairway, he looked just the same whether he had just had three birdies in a row or a couple of double bogeys. Inside, it may have been a different matter, as at Troon, but Locke believed in showing no emotion, either joy or pain.

In part he had learned this from the equally impassive Ben Hogan and he had also noted that Hogan seldom talked on the course, just a very occasional remark to his partner. Locke followed suit, not allowing his eyes to meet those of spectators and side-stepping any attempt at conversation with the remark, 'I'll see you later in the clubhouse'. Preserving his concentration was one of the South African's key assets. Another was relaxation. When due to play, Locke always arrived with time to spare and, in between putting a sock on or lacing a shoe, would often pause to chat or to tell a story. Although in his youth a great practiser, the mature Locke did little. Peter Thomson once said to me: 'You know, Peter, I never saw Bobby hit more than a few putts on a practice green before he went out.' As regards warming up, I remember seeing Locke and his old caddie Bill Golder with half-a-dozen balls and a wedge in his hand before the last round of the 1957 Open Championship by the putting green at St Andrews. I paused to talk and eventually Locke walked to the 1st tee without having hit one of them away. At most he only wanted to check that the machinery was still in order and he made do this time with a couple of swings. Practice before a round was tiring and he wanted to conserve his energy.

Out on the course he aimed to stay as relaxed as possible. He walked rather slowly and liked to let his arms hang loosely at his side. In both Europe and the States there were complaints about his slow pace but Locke maintained that he did not delay once he reached his ball. He had decided on both club and the kind of shot he wanted to play as he walked up; an easy practice swing and he played the shot. It wasn't only that rather funereal progress that made Locke instantly recognizable on the golf course. Like many other golfers, he had his trademarks. As a gesture to showmanship, he always wore a white cap. His shoes too were always white and were made of buckskin with leather soles. He wore navy blue plus fours both because they were comfortable and because they were traditional golfing attire. The outfit was completed by a white shirt and club tie, the latter because it made him feel completely correct.

Locke's next Open Championship victory came in 1952, when, incidentally, the Australian Norman von Nida complained that Locke's slowness was holding up play. Locke had lost three holes on the pair ahead but blamed poor crowd control. By this time, the Australian Peter Thomson was his main rival but Locke managed to play the steadier golf. Thomson's great finish of three birdies and five pars was not quite good enough. Locke got home by a stroke to make it three wins in four years, a feat only achieved by James Braid and Harry Vardon since the turn of the century.

From this time on, Bobby was a slightly less dominant figure in championships, though he continued to be as formidable as ever in tournament play, winning eight events, for example, in 1954. He was still far and away the best player South Africa had ever produced and perhaps the first really world-class golfer from outside Britain and the USA. In his native land he was almost unbeatable. Between 1935 and 1955, he won the South African Open nine times and the Matchplay Championship seven, as well as a host of state events, all before there was a real tour in South Africa.

If Locke had looked about 40 years old since the end of the Second World War, as the 1957 Open began at St Andrews he was nearly there in reality. By then considered past his best, Locke came to the championship on good form, with two wins in his last three outings but facing a Peter Thomson who had won the championship three years in a row. Up with the leaders all the way, Locke countered a 69 from Thomson in the second round with his own 68 on the final morning. It gave him a three-stroke lead over Thomson and the Scotsman Eric Brown, who had led earlier. Thomson was out first. He looked the man likely to set a target and indeed he did with a final round of 70, which included a few putts missed from about 4 feet. Despite the tension that he had come to feel increasingly with the passing of the years, Locke played throughout with apparent composure and he always managed to preserve his lead, coming in with a round of 70, a total of 279 and a win over Thomson by three strokes.

Locke had always said he wanted to retire with a fortune made at the age of 40 and he'd done it. After that year, he continued to compete but seldom featured. I think he was content.

LOCKE, ARTHUR D'ARCY
Born: Germiston, Transvaal, South Africa, 20 November 1917
Major championship victories: 1949 British Open Championship;
1950 British Open Championship; 1952 British Open
Championship; 1957 British Open Championship.
US Tour victories (1947–50): 11
European Tour victories (1938–57): 23
Other overseas victories: 5
South Africa: 38

PETER
THOMSON

Many golfers, good and poor alike, make golf far too complicated for their own good. My father, Percy Alliss, used to say that golf was a simple game and that it was golfers who made it complicated. This could not be said, however, of the Australian, Peter Thomson. Of our superstars, he stands alone as a man who really does think that golf is a simple game. You need touch, not muscle, and must just solve the main problems of the game. All you have to do is hit your tee-shot onto the fairway, the next one on the green and then don't three-putt.

Thomson is undoubtedly, a splendid golf writer, and also a great player of the game. His book, co-authored with a journalist, *This Wonderful World of Golf*, is unusual in that Thomson's contributions are kept separate from his co-author's, Desmond Zwar. There's no doubt in my mind that what Peter has to say is penetrating and economically expressed. Unlike almost every other champion, Peter has never written a book of golf instruction, even though there has been no lack of offers to do so. He feels, as did Gene Sarazen before him, that there just isn't enough worth saying. Just as you won't find on the shelves of your local bookshop vast tomes on the 'how to' of cricket or baseball, Thomson feels that there is no mystique about golf. Aim, draw it back, fire and think clearly.

These beliefs certainly were enormously helpful to his golf game, one of the most effective of modern times. Perhaps Peter was honest enough to admit to himself that his own method was not quite perfect. The grip with his left hand is much too strong, his head dips into the hitting area and there is some lateral movement. The right-hand position, though quite acceptable, has the V made by thumb and forefinger directly pointing to his right shoulder, a much stronger position than that used by most other good players of the modern era.

The great flaw in Thomson's record was that he achieved so little in the United States. In 1956 he won his only US tournament, the Texas Open, and that same year finished among the top ten money winners. He also had his best placing in the US Open, fourth, four strokes behind the winner, Cary Middlecoff. In the US Masters, his best finish was fifth in 1957, not surprising in that the Augusta National is the championship course least suited to the Australian's abilities.

It wasn't only the architecture of the Augusta course that was a problem. Thomson's type of game also put him at a disadvantage on most US tournament lay-outs where it is golfers who hit long highflighted drives – with a few exceptions, including a Hogan – who benefit. Also at an advantage are those who prefer 'target golf', hitting irons flat out to the flag, knowing the shot will pull up very rapidly. In Thomson's domination of the British Open during the 1950s, strategic shots to the fairway, superb touch, judgement of distance and an ability to predict the run of the ball were the key features of his golfing armoury. However, in the States his conservative driving was a drawback and his feel for the running of the ball little use.

This bunker shot finished close. Note the Australian's strong left-hand grip with the right in a weak position

Thomson was not a particularly long hitter and thought of driving very much in terms of placing his ball in the best position for the shot to the green. He was fully prepared to concede even more length by using no more than a 3-wood during many of his tournaments and championships. You could always do something from the fairway, he felt, but not the deep rough – all very different from the thoughts of Seve Ballesteros. He had considerable distaste for target golf. Brought up on often baked, running, Melbourne courses, he quickly came to enjoy the fairly similar challenge of British seaside links. In Thomson's great years, links greens frequently didn't hold even the most sweetly-struck iron shots so the player needed to judge where to place the shot so that it ran the last 50 or 60 yards up to the flag over the bumps and through the hollows.

Even so, there was more to Thomson's lack of success in the States than that. His approach to the game of golf strongly resembles Bobby Locke's. The South African triumphed; the Australian, let's make no bones about it, failed. Questioned about it today, Peter is apt to remark that he was pitted against some rather good players with such names as Snead, Hogan,

Demaret and Mangrum. Never quick to praise, his admiration for Ben Hogan is extreme. He once wrote: 'He would play a whole tournament, sometimes for four days, without a single bad shot. For this reason, I would say that there couldn't possibly have been a greater player in the history of golf.'

It's interesting to see how Thomson rates the avoidance of bad shots far more highly than brilliance. So do I, even if a little reluctantly. Of course the superb shots are the ones that remain bright in the memory for many a year but drives off the fairway, the occasional poor pitch shot and careless putt have much more effect on a tournament result. It's all, however, in tune with the basic Thomson philosophy: it's a simple game but we mustn't expect perfection. Make the most of your talents.

Sometimes it's unbelievable that they don't go in

I've been a little severe in virtually writing off Peter Thomson as a competitor in the USA, but a little tongue in cheek. By one of the oddities of our strange game, the great Australian, in his fifty-sixth year, became a great success in the USA.

It all came about on the US Senior Tour, which only really got going as recently as 1980. Thomson made his first entry in 1982 and won some $30,000 that year. In 1983 he almost doubled his winnings and seemed to me to be honing his game once more to full competitive sharpness, even practising for a couple of hours a week. Towards the end of 1984 he came into a new American Kingdom. In September 1984, he won the World Seniors' Invitational by one stroke from Arnold Palmer with scores of 69, 69, 69 and 74. This was his first Seniors' win and his first in the States for 28 years. He followed it up by winning five of the next nine events and, in May 1985, had won four of his last five entries, and nine in all by the autumn.

In his mid-fifties, Peter had become a name in the States, almost certain to become leading money winner in 1985 with more than $120,000 banked by early May, a figure he was soon to double by the end of July and then cruise past $300,000, eclipsing previous records. So why was Thomson doing so much better in middle age than 30 years earlier against such great names as Arnold Palmer, Billy Casper, Don January, Miller Barber and Gene Littler? I think he has maintained his easy rhythmic method, losing, for example, very little length since his greatest days. Some, like Arnold Palmer, for instance, who make a far more explosive golf swing, have suffered more dramatically from the passing of years. Even more importantly, his nerve and touch for putting are still intact.

He clearly relishes this late success and, though he retired from serious competitive golf several years ago, has since become fully committed to the US Senior Tour, declaring he would play almost all the possible events in 1985, a rather stiffer schedule than the one handled by, for example, Tom Watson and Jack Nicklaus on the main tour.

Obviously, he has retained his appetite for playing golf and competing into what is almost old age for a golfer and remember that Thomson has been doing it for 35 years and more which is enough to dull most palates! He seems to be getting his second wind. When the situations get tougher his golf brain still gets sharper and eye clearer: he is in charge of mind and body. Undoubtedly, the simplicity of his approach to the strategy of the game has helped enormously. His thoughts on the golf swing are equally simple. Although Peter has written little on golf instruction, he's certainly talked to me and many others about his ideas.

Perhaps the most central one is the importance of the set-up, recognized by all as vital today but much less so in Peter's young days, when many stars were unorthodox in both grip and set-up. For wood shots he believes the ball should be opposite the front heel, distance from the body being governed by extending the left arm straight, but not rigid. With toes parallel to the target line, Thomson is at right angles to the line of shot.

However, there's still the right hand to be put on the grip. Here, the player needs think only of reaching *under*, causing the right shoulder to be set lower. So many golfers destroy their whole set-up by reaching *round*. This means that the left and right shoulders move towards the left. The hips follow in sympathy. It all twists the top half of the body left of target. The essentials of shoulders, hips and arms all being along the target line is destroyed by that one wrong movement. Depending on the position of the club face at the moment of impact, only a slice or pull can result.

If these ideas are simple, Thomson's thoughts on the grip are even more pithy. He believes that the position of the hands on the club merely follow body position and has identical thoughts to Bobby Locke as regards firmness. At the beginning of the backswing, the club must be held lightly, the fingers merely tight enough to stop the club dropping from the fingers.

An ideally relaxed position on the follow-through. The late Tom Haliburton watches

Thereafter, the grip tightens instinctively, reaching a maximum at and after impact. He sees the backswing as a natural movement. There's no need to think of any of the detailed body movements. You just draw the club straight back and everything else will fall neatly and inevitably into place. How far back, you may well ask. As far as comfortable, replies Thomson. Swinging back to the ball, Thomson felt, should be seen merely a matter of accelerating the clubhead through the ball, with no thought of actually hitting at it.

Of course, these beliefs didn't always produce the right results for the great Australian. Did he then follow the time-honoured pattern of the long and lonely hours on the practice ground? Not a bit of it. If Thomson found, for example, that his tendency to draw the ball had become a nasty sharp hook, as the first move, he'd sit down in an armchair to think about it. What had gone wrong with his simple mechanism, the very few factors he felt mattered? Usually he came up with an answer quite quickly. Time to go out to the practice ground. There he'd test out the 'cure', which was really no more than a return to his basic method. A few shots followed. As often as not the solution worked and Thomson went back home or to his hotel. If it didn't, he went back and thought again.

All this was also typical of Thomson's attitude to practice in general. He believed this should be over and done with before a tournament began. During it, you just warmed up before a round. For Thomson this meant hitting no more than a couple of shots with each club and rounding off by teeing up a couple of balls and hitting them away with driver or 3-wood. As he once wrote: 'In this way I kept an open but keen expectant mind on the task ahead. I have never thought it worth wasting energy in concentration on practice before a round. It might be in short supply by the end of the day.' Just like Bobby Jones?

Indeed, just as much as Jack Nicklaus years later, Thomson believed that winning was a product of the mind rather than swing. Nicklaus called it 'course management'; Thomson declared: 'Championships are only partly played on the green grass. Most of it is decided in the mind and the human mind is capable of any human contrariness.' He thought that success did not come from perfection as a result of repetitive practice but from learning how to compete. 'Target practice,' he once said, 'doesn't make you a good guerrilla.' The ability to win, and compete, Thomson felt, had to be in-born. It couldn't be learned except that a particular player may need time to learn to bring out what latent talent he has within him. Of course, there are exceptions, the players who felt they were not prepared unless they had paid their dues on the practice grounds and putting greens of the world.

We see this particular theme repeated throughout this book – the avid practisers and the Thomsons. Of the former, we have, for example, Hogan, Player, Cotton and Nicklaus. At the other extreme with Thomson himself, are Bobby Locke and Walter Hagen. Others fall into a midway group, the golfers who spend lonely hours in developing their golf game and thereafter tend just to hit a few balls off before going to the 1st tee, perhaps mostly to reassure themselves that their basic swing is still in good order, rhythm good and muscles loose.

Thomson's lonely hours were spent in Australia during the Second World War. Like certain other Supreme Champions he was largely self-taught. Through the War, he 'hacked away' and slowly 'got the hang of it'. In his own words: 'There was nobody to instruct me or *put me wrong*.' That phrase in italics says quite a lot about Peter Thomson. He was a loner who has always preferred to find his own salvation. The ideas of others, like as not, would 'put him wrong'. As a competitor too he follows his own path. He plays his golf, and disappears. Thomson is aware that there are only 24 hours in a day, less 8 hours for sleeping. The 16 left shouldn't just be devoted to golf, playing it and talking about it. Five hours for all that are quite enough.

There's another world outside the current tournament and Thomson has always liked to seek it out. This might mean a walk in the Cairngorms, visits to art galleries, the opera and museums, a good book or just a walk about looking at whatever takes his fancy.

His diversity of interests have made him knowledgeable and entertaining. I'd far rather spend a month with Peter than a full day with one or two others who shall remain nameless!

Having, as he put it, 'hacked about' through the War, Thomson had a single-figure handicap by the end of it and in 1949 turned pro, to the disapproval of some of his family. He didn't have a distinguished career behind him though he had finished leading amateur in the 1948 Australian Open. As a professional, however, he was soon on his way, finishing second in the 1950 Australian Open and the same year becoming New Zealand Open Champion. In a sense, this was Thomson's best event. Between his first win and his last in 1971, he was nine-times champion, a feat comparable to those of Locke and Player in the South African Open. Oddly, his further successes in Australia were rather limited. He took only two more Australian Opens and a handful of other important Australian events. But if Thomson was not a dominant force in his own land, he was certainly one of the most effective international golfers in the same way as Player and Ballesteros were to become in later years.

Thomson, indeed, was very interested in the idea of a true world tour being developed, where golfers would move, stage by stage around the globe, following the seasons in both East and West. Perhaps this will still come. He helped set up the now thriving Asian Circuit. How well I remember talking through his ideas 25 years and more ago. He had victories in Japan and Asia but perhaps was at his best in Europe, where I believe he really preferred to play, just like Bobby Locke.

Thomson made a good impression on his first appearance in the 1951 British Open at Royal Portrush, finishing in sixth place. The following year, he made an even greater impact, second behind Locke by just one stroke at Royal Lytham. He had to be content with the same placing behind Ben Hogan at Carnoustie in 1953 and by then it was obvious that Thomson was a new star ready to take the centre of the stage. That came in 1954 at Royal Birkdale and this time it was Locke, his great rival for the next few years, who finished in second place.

Thomson had begun a period of dominance in the British Open at least equal to that of Young Tom Morris about 90 years before and not bettered even by Tom Watson in the 1970s and 1980s. From 1952 to 1958, he was always either first or second. When Gary Player's turn came in 1959, it didn't seem in the natural order of things that Peter Thomson should be well down the finishers, ten strokes behind the winner. But before this happened, Thomson had won three British Opens in a row and four in five years, Locke making his memorable last charge at St Andrews in 1957. It's easy to win when your game is at a peak but Peter could still do it when in relatively poor form. Others might do their career best but still found he was first past the tape. He could handle the pressure and never threw a championship away. With pars needed to win, he did it.

Although the dominance now seems almost total there remains a statistical oddity: his wins were all by fairly narrow margins: one stroke in 1954; two in 1955; three in 1956; and a play-off win over David Thomas in 1958. By making this point, I in no way intend to undermine his achievement. It's easy enough to win by a mile when your game is at a peak and everything running your way. Obviously, Thomson's game wasn't at such a peak throughout this period. Indeed, he wasn't by any means a frequent winner of other events in the 1950s. The British Open brought out the best in him. He raised his game and contrived to be first past the post.

Why? Well, his game was ideally suited to links golf on hard ground – almost invariable in July. In such conditions he's been described as the greatest manipulator of the small 1.62 ball ever. But there was a still more vital factor. Thomson could handle the pressure better than the rest. Observers at the time always commented on his composure. He went on his way smiling and quickly, the swing and set-up always rhythmical and beautifully balanced.

After that 1959 Muirfield 'disaster', Thomson became even more successful world wide, but especially so in Europe. His career total is 26 which compares with any other player since (or even before) the Second World War. How successful he was can be seen partly in terms of money winnings, more than £71,000 in days before the big prizes came. Thomson's career and my own covered much the same years – the beginning of the 1950s to the end of the 1960s – and with 20 major victories I earned £28,000. That's less than is sometimes now on offer for one event.

With the arrival of Arnold Palmer on the British golf scene in 1960, Thomson became rather a forgotten man in the Open Championship. The

In 1956 at Hoylake. Peter became the only man to win three Open Championships in a row this century

American's great deeds in 1961 and 1962 made him a folk hero. Thomson played well enough in those years but a bad round seemed to slip in – even a 77 in 1962. Then in 1963 at Royal Lytham he began with rounds of 67 and 69, but faded right away in the last round to a 78. At St Andrews the following year, he self-destructed in the first round with a 79. Heads were shaking sadly. The great champion was gone. Not so for me, his greatest achievement lay just ahead. Thomson's Open Championships had all come his way against very strong international fields – but with the exception of the Americans. After the days of Jones, Sarazen and Hagen it was suddenly not fashionable to cross the Atlantic for the Open. It took time and money and the prize money was poor. Some still did but on average no more than a couple of real stars every year.

By 1965, this had all changed. Palmer had led the return and his example was quickly followed by Jack Nicklaus, Doug Sanders, Phil Rodgers and Tony Lema, among others. Nicklaus was the phenomenon of the age, Palmer still at his best and Tony Lema was one of the Big Four. Lema had dazzled British eyes at St Andrews in 1964 with his command of a strong field. Before play began at Birkdale in 1965, the talk was all about these players. Thomson began with a 74, to trail Lema by six strokes and Palmer by four but he hit back the second day with a finely-played 68 to be just two behind Lema and one worse than Palmer.

To British spectators, this was a new Thomson. Normally smiling and with time for a word with the crowds, he was now stern and silent. For the final day's 36 holes he was paired with Tony Lema and had caught him after nine holes. In a stiff breeze, Thomson was round in 72 in the morning, compared to 75s from both Palmer and Lema. A 77 from Nicklaus put him right out of it. In the afternoon Thomson played steadily, reaching the turn in 34 but then began a sequence of missed putts. Nevertheless he retained a one-stroke lead over Tony Lema with a few holes left to play. (Palmer was on his way to a 79.)

The last two holes at Birkdale that year both measured more than 500 yards. Thomson needed to finish 4, 4 to be virtually certain of the championship. On both holes he drove straight and then threaded running long-irons to the heart of both greens before safely two-putting, while Lema collapsed to a 5, 6 finish. Surely this was his finest hour.

I'm very honoured to count Peter Thomson among my friends and have much in common with him, particularly the belief that golf is just a part of life. In this respect, we can see strong differences among our golf heroes. For Thomson, it was a job of work which had to be pursued with a relentless selfishness. Perhaps this led to the break-down of his first marriage to the delightful Lois (by whom he had a daughter, Deidre) about the end of the 1950s. He soon married again and has three more children, all now into their twenties.

Thomson faced retirement from tournament golf without sentimentality and in due course, towards the end of the 1970s, announced that he had played his last Australian Open. He began to seek other ways to exploit his energies, which were already occupied in golf architecture. But, as I've said, Peter had wider interests than these in golf, to which he had already added administration through his own PGA, as president for many years.

He tried politics in his home state and came quite close to being elected and also involved himself in campaigns against drug addiction. Obviously, he had put competing in tournament golf behind him for ever until the news came over the bush telegraph that gold had been discovered on the US Senior Tour ... He is taking it home by the sackful and when his winnings start to dwindle, as they must through the ageing process, Thomson will think it over and stop competing. Life has plenty to offer outside golf. On the Seniors Tour, he has set records that will be very hard to break.

THOMSON, PETER W., CBE
Born: Melbourne, Victoria, Australia, 23 August 1929
Major championship victories: 1954 British Open Championship;
1955 British Open Championship; 1956 British Open
Championship; 1958 British Open Championship; 1965 British Open
Championship
US Tour victories (1956–72) 1
European Tour victories (1956–72): 26
Australasia victories (1950–72): 19
Asia and Japan victories (1954–76): 11
European Tour money winnings: £71,400

ARNOLD

PALMER

In February 1973 Arnold Palmer won the Bob Hope Desert Classic for the fifth time, beating Jack Nicklaus and Johnny Miller by a couple of strokes. It was wet and blustery, but Palmer said: 'For me, the sun was out all day.' It was his sixty-first victory on the US Tour – and also his last. Well why not, you might well ask. After all, he was 43, a fair age for a golfer with the wear and tear of some 18 years on the US Tour behind him.

Even so, his failure to win again is all part of the Palmer enigma. Perhaps more than any other player of comparable stature, except Snead, Arnold remained desperately eager to play and still is, a dozen years later. So many others, some very talented, have wearied of it all, hating to compete and even to play the game at all – Byron Nelson, Dave Hill and Tom Weiskopf in the States and Brian Barnes, Bernard Hunt and Dave Thomas in Britain, all Ryder Cup players and notable examples of this attitude. They have either given up or soldiered on reluctantly, wishing they weren't on a golf course.

Palmer has continued to be keen to win and has had his successes since 1973. In 1975, for instance, he won the Spanish Open at La Manga and the PGA Championship in foul conditions at Sandwich. His last victory outside the US Seniors Tour came in 1980 when he won the Canadian PGA, though not against a top-class field. However, his decline in performance since 1973 is really not in the least surprising. By that time he had reached an age when some falling-away in skills is just about inevitable. It's astonishing, though, to realize how a man who piled up a series of major championship victories over quite a short period from 1958–64, continued to feature often – yet he never won another after 1964. Then despite the menacing presence of Jack Nicklaus, so many more victories in the majors seemed likely, even certain.

What went wrong? Basically, the putting more than anything else. Palmer was a man who always went for the back of the hole – people even said he knocked it out of shape. For several years, he was hardly ever short, confident that he could knock in the 4- and 6-footers he might leave himself on the way back. Gradually that self-belief disappeared. Palmer became more concerned to get the approach putts dead instead of threatening the hole. As a result, it brought added pressure on his pitching. With his new attitude, he had to get his approaches close so that his more tentative putting could still produce birdies or save pars. Alas, always a great chipper, Palmer was never a good bunker player or pitcher. Perhaps all this called for a subtlety and feel that wasn't really in Palmer's golfing make-up. Essentially he was a crash, bang golfer on every shot. It may seem almost silly to bracket, say, driving, chipping and putting but, if you think about it and watch, perhaps you'll come to agree with me that it's just possible golfers at all levels almost always shade into two categories: those who make a forceful stroke at the ball and the others who you sense trying to feel in their fingers the pace and run of the shot.

The key ingredients in Arnold Palmer's game were long driving, mastery of the long-irons, bold putting and reasonable mid-iron play. From sand and, say 80 yards in, he was never more than competent. He also had that one vital ingredient, which is confidence bordering on arrogance. More than anything else, it made him both a great player and the greatest crowd puller since Jones and Hagen, perhaps ever.

Palmer began as a very good college player at Wake Forest and then went into the US Coast Guard. He first appeared on the national stage when he won the 1954 US Amateur Championship. Shortly afterwards, he turned pro and was almost immediately successful, winning the 1955 Canadian Open. That first year, he finished thirty-second in the US Tour money list but moved up a gear in 1956, taking four tournaments. He did the same the following year. These were achievements which today would put a player top of the money list but that was not the case then. He had not yet found the limelight.

Palmer really arrived in 1958, a year in which he won only three events but one of these was the US Masters. He produced no real fireworks but

Near the 1st tee at
Portmarnock in 1960 —
I see no ships!

found himself with the green jacket when both Doug Ford and Fred Hawkins missed birdie putts on the last green to force a play-off. It's odd to think now that Palmer, at 28, the age when Bobby Jones retired, had become the youngest champion in almost 30 years. They start winning even sooner now and perhaps burn out more quickly.

Palmer became accepted as a great player in 1960. Besides six wins in tournaments, he won two of the major championships and created a sensation in another that he didn't win. With the US Masters, a legend was born. Palmer had led each day with rounds of 67, 73 and 72 but he came to the last two holes a stroke behind Ken Venturi. He birdied both, a very unusual feat at Augusta, to win by a stroke. This was the beginning of the widely-accepted belief, part of his legend, that Arnie could always produce the shots when they really counted. Of course, none of us can. That perfectly struck and judged 8-iron may always skip past the flag a little more than anyone could have anticipated or bite, and spin back way short of target. We play golf in the most natural surroundings of any game. It's no snooker table. Part of golf is hitting the perfect shot and hoping, yes hoping, the ball will behave itself – the difference can be 2 inches or 20 yards.

A couple of months later, Palmer was at Cherry Hills, Denver, for the US Open, six victories already behind him that year. He was the favourite but Mike Souchak quickly put that into perspective with opening rounds of 68 and 67. Arnold trailed eight strokes behind, apparently not in contention. Souchak then faltered a little, taking 73 but Palmer's 72 made up very little ground indeed. Obviously, it wasn't going to be his year. But Palmer, with the confidence of all those wins behind him, had other thoughts. A last round of 65 might do it. Easier said than done. No one that year had bettered Souchak's 67 and, a good many years later, when the US Open returned to Cherry Hills, scoring was higher. During the lunch break, he told American journalist Bob Drum about the possibilities. Drum promised Palmer a fizzy drink, out of turn, if he did it.

Palmer thought one key to playing the course was to get a drive onto the green at the 1st hole, a par-4. In trying to do just that, he was already three over par on the hole for the championship with his three previous attempts. This time, his drive, savagely struck, bounded through the collar of rough short of the green and he two-putted for his birdie. He had thought he might manage a 65. Confidence thrives on an early boost and Arnold went on to birdie the next three holes. With a couple more before the turn, he had caught the field, was out in 30 strokes and, almost inconceivably, the championship was within reach. There were no more fireworks. Palmer parred his way home. Jack Nicklaus couldn't quite manage to be the last amateur to win the US Open nor could Ben Hogan take the title for a record fifth time, his own last charge. What an extraordinary feat that 65 was and it certainly fuelled the legend that Arnold could produce shots at will.

On, then, to St Andrews, for the Centenary Open. Although few Americans had entered that year, like Hogan seven years before, Palmer had listened when told that a golfer must win the British Open to earn golfing immortality. What was more, he had a strong chance, with the Masters and the US Open already in the bag, of doing the professional Grand Slam of the four major championships in one year.

Palmer began tidily enough. Despite three-putting the feared Road hole in his first two rounds, he had scores of 70 and 71, yet this left him seven strokes behind the great Argentine, Roberto de Vicenzo, whose start of two 67s was the second best total ever achieved. Ahead of Palmer by five was the little-fancied Australian, Kel Nagle. De Vicenzo was a majestic player who had come close many times; Nagle was steadiness and grit personified. The third round used to be thought decisive in a championship, though things have now changed. We tend to think of play over the last few holes as usually settling the outcome. Palmer had a round of 70. It left him four behind the Australian but he had nearly caught de Vicenzo, who had a rather poorly played round of 75. Nevertheless, he was to remain at the top of the leader board until he faded away on the last nine in the afternoon.

Despite the gap between Palmer and Nagle, the American was highly tipped to win as the last round began. The British public were quick to warm to the drama of his play: the boldness of both his shots directly at the flag and putting. In comparison, Nagle seemed rather a dull fellow and few seemed to notice that he always kept the ball in play and never three-putted, a disciple of Peter Thomson, in fact, who had backed him to win. Playing just ahead of Nagle, Palmer soon announced his intentions by pitching dead at both the 1st and 2nd, a 3, 3 start. But the Australian had birdies of his own on the outward nine and both reached the turn in 34. So the gap remained at four strokes, with Palmer trying everything he knew to close it. At the 13th, he had a birdie and drew up to Nagle's rear wheel when the Australian dropped a stroke.

The Road Hole always plays a big part in a St Andrews' Open Championship and the year of 1960 was no exception. Many think it the most difficult hole in golf, a supreme test of both placement of the drive and precision of shot into the green. This is long, narrow and open only after a tee-shot down the right hand side which must flirt with an out-of-bounds corner and come to rest as close as the player dares to a further stretch of out of bounds. If you drive more safely left, the green becomes an almost impossible target to both hit and hold. It's set across your line of shot, protected by the Road bunker, with the road itself just beyond the green.

Palmer did not drive all that well, going too far left, and then played towards the front of the green. From there he succeeded in getting down in a chip and a putt. It was 'only' a par but his first there during the championship. It must have felt like a birdie and it increased the pressure on Nagle behind.

At the last hole, Palmer increased it further. His drive came to rest on Granny Clark's Wynd, a road which crosses the fairway. Palmer clipped it away neatly, his pitch finishing only about 5 feet from the hole. His closing birdie for a 68 had given him a chance of the championship, was certainly a grandstand finish and began the Palmer legend in Britain. But it wasn't to be. Nagle finished undaunted with two pars and was champion by a single stroke. Palmer, however, had enjoyed the experience and vowed to return. He has done so nearly every year to this day.

By this time, Palmer had just about reached the mid-point of his greatest years. At the 1961 US Masters, it was a Player-Palmer battle all the way and it reached an almost comical conclusion. Player came to the last hole just ahead of Arnold and bunkered his second shot to the right of the green. As all good professionals are supposed to do, he then got down in two more for a total of 280. Minutes later, Palmer, who had played a strong last round after starting four strokes behind Gary, found himself in the same bunker. He needed a 4 for a 69 and a one-stroke victory and a 5 to force a play-off. Instead, he gave the championship to Player, taking a horrifying four strokes more to get down from 25 yards. His bunker shot flew through the green and his chip back was strong. But perhaps he'd really lost it a few minutes earlier when he had lost concentration on his shot to the green, relaxing because he had overhauled Gary.

Not raining, not blowing a gale but you can see how much Palmer's gallery trust the weather during the 1961 British Open at Royal Birkdale

Arnold Palmer with his wife
Winnie after his first British
Open victory in 1961. A truly
great combination

Not long after, he came to Royal Birkdale for his second British Open
– and once more the legend grew. It was typical English summery weather
on the first day – occasional sunshine and frequent rain, wind and thunder.
Even so, there were plenty of scores of 71 or better. There was no such
variety in the weather on the second day. It was the last great gale of the
championship, perhaps the equal of Sandwich in 1938. Palmer began in
the worst of it and played one of the greatest short bursts of golf ever seen.
Boring his long-irons low under the full force of the wind, he managed to
birdie five of the first six holes. Those who saw him declare that they've
never seen anything like it before or since. Even Palmer couldn't quite
maintain that pace but was still one under par for his round, which
included a 7 near the end after his ball moved when he was about to play
out of a bunker. The result was a thinned effort right across the green and
a penalty stroke as well.

After a day's break because of flooded greens, play resumed on the
Saturday for the normal 36 holes. In the morning, Palmer had a 69 and
took the lead by a stroke from the late Dai Rees. Again, there had been

the occasional minor miracle. At the 16th, then 510 yards, Palmer saw his third shot sail away rightwards towards the out of bounds on the very strong wind. It came down a few feet short in very dense rough at the foot of some willow scrub. It was no time for subtleties. He opened up the face of his wedge and lashed into, and through, everything. The ball soared high and (there was a deal of luck in this) came to rest right by the hole. At Birkdale, they say the scars he left behind remained for a year or more.

In the final round, Palmer increased his lead all the way. Later, a plaque was erected to commemorate a shot he played on the 15th. He pushed his drive on this 381-yard hole into deep rough but again strength of forearm and hand enabled him to carve a 6-iron through to the ball and force it onto the green. Only Bobby Jones and Arnold have been so honoured for Open Championship shots.

Such power was the main impression Palmer left on spectators in his peak years. Surely no one thought his swing was elegant. Henry Cotton was particularly disparaging, remarking that Arnold never seemed to finish in the same position twice running and was always off balance at the finish of his swing. There was some truth in that last point. If a player is capable of hitting with really tremendous power, the sheer momentum will cause a kind of recoil at the end of his follow-through, as you can see today when Seve Ballesteros hits full out. What matters, however, is that the player is balanced through the hitting area. No one could fault Palmer here.

In fact, there's a great deal to admire in Palmer's swing and technique. Its foundation, the grip, is ideal with the hands aligned palm to palm and the Vs pointing about midway between chin and right shoulder. The take-away is one piece and quite fast, as is the rest of Palmer's backswing. He retains full control because of those exceptionally strong hands and forearms and, wild though he appeared to be, hit far more fairways than most and became a superb driver of the ball. The finish is unusual, the clubhead sometimes pointing on high rather than the more relaxed over-the-shoulder position of a Snead or Little. This is because Palmer is normally concerned not to miss shots on the left and therefore slashes his right hand through the hitting area, striving to hold the clubface square, rather than allow it to turn over shut. That old wives' tale of 'too much right hand' doesn't in fact produce a hook with a Palmer technique. It's letting the clubhead turn over too soon which does that.

So perhaps those early observers were wrong when they thought Palmer had a 'bad swing' and tended to put down much of his success to fearless putting. But he did have areas of weakness. As I've said elsewhere, many power hitters can become all delicacy on the greens but be relatively poor at finessing shots when they've missed a green or are bunkered. They become comparatively inaccurate when playing a soft shot or judging the run of the ball. Of course, this is still just a matter of degree. Palmer didn't get the ball as close to the hole as many others but then had the putting

Arnie in his forties giving it a real 'go'

equalizer which set him apart for several years: he never seemed to miss a short one and holed far more than his fair share from medium and long range.

In 1962 Palmer had another very good year. In the US Masters there was a tie with Gary Player and Dow Finsterwald. In the 18-hole play-off, Palmer was three strokes behind the South African going into the second nine but 31 back gave him his third Masters – making him only the third to achieve this after the late Jimmy Demaret and Sam Snead.

In the US Open, he tied for first place with Jack Nicklaus but then lost the play-off, forfeiting what could well have been a very good chance indeed of the professional Grand Slam for soon after he was to play perhaps his greatest major championship. This was the British Open at Troon. The course was well-nigh unplayable, a dusty arena where the ball bounced hither and thither without logic. The same shot to a green might stop short or bound and skip 20 yards through. A drive to mid-fairway, catching a knob, might race away sideways into bush or deep rough. The latter happened to Palmer in a practice round and he seriously considered flying back home then and there. He thought the damned course was unplayable.

When the championship began, the recent US Open Champion, Jack Nicklaus almost failed to qualify. He had an 80 in his first round, which included a 10 on the very difficult 11th hole and only survived the cut because he followed with a 72 the next day. By that time a repeat of the 1960 Palmer-Nagle duel was very much in prospect. Arnold had followed a 71 with a 69 to lead the Australian by two. For the 36 holes of the final day they were paired. Quickly Nagle caught him and went ahead but Palmer then produced an unblemished flow of magnificent strokes to be round in 67 for a five-stroke lead. He finished off with his third round under 70 to win the title by six strokes from a man who had done little wrong. The third-placed man was thirteen strokes behind Palmer's total of 276 and the man who had beaten him in the US Open play-off, Jack Nicklaus, was twenty-nine strokes behind.

That was Palmer's last success in the British Open, an eclipse that would be comparable today, say, to Tom Watson and Seve Ballesteros never featuring again. Palmer had also won his only US Open but there was a Masters title still to come when he achieved his fourth Green Jacket in 1964. This was as emphatic as Troon, with the same six-stroke margin and also three rounds under 70.

One major championship which was still missing from his record was the US PGA. He once produced four rounds under 70 and was still second, three strokes behind and had two other second-place finishes. During Palmer's great spell from the 1958 to 1964 Masters, he won 7 of the 25 majors held and threatened to win several more.

No more came his way. However, if a sudden decline, it was by no means total. He remained a force in the US Masters, being second in 1965, and fourth in 1966 and 1967. He came close in four more US Opens, by far and away the most remarkable being 1966 at Olympic Country Club just outside San Francisco. After three rounds he had a three-stroke lead and was paired with Billy Casper. Palmer then stormed to the turn in 32 to be seven strokes ahead, with Casper thinking mainly of making sure of second place and playing safe from the tee and aiming other shots to the wide parts of the greens.

Palmer's thoughts were more of the US Open record. If he could get home in 36 over the last nine that would be good enough to break Ben Hogan's record 276. With four holes to go, it looked as if he might do it, though he was a stroke over par on the back nine. Casper still lagged five strokes behind. The 15th at Olympic is a fairly comfortable par-3 in all conscience, just 150 yards. Palmer missed the green with a 7-iron and was bunkered, eventually taking 4. Casper got a 2. It was the first time Palmer had given him a thought. His lead was cut to three. Said Palmer later: 'That's when I began to wonder. I know what can happen in golf.'

The 16th is a very long hole of just over 600 yards. If Casper was now going for victory there was no sign of it. With a long drive needed to increase the chances of a birdie he played safe with an iron from the tee. Palmer's drive then clattered into a cypress tree and down into thick rye grass. Palmer debated whether to play back to the fairway with a lofted iron but eventually made the perilous decision to go for distance with a long-iron. He slashed at his ball but it only fizzed through the long grass and came to rest just some 70 yards further on. He was still about 350 yards from the green and did very well to get down in four more for a 6. Casper, meanwhile, got himself safely on in three and then holed a medium-length putt for a birdie. That really set the cat amongst the pigeons. Casper had pulled up, playing cautiously for second place, to within a stroke of the leader, while Palmer made all the mistakes.

On the 17th, Palmer was again in the rough and again dropped a stroke. They came to the final hole all square and everything to play for. Palmer once more hooked into the rough but this time managed to get his par, as did Billy Casper, though both had to hole testing putts on the last green – especially Palmer. In the 18-hole play-off the next day, Palmer still had his chances of winning. He went to the turn in 33 to be two ahead but his lead went on the 12th where both were in trouble with their tee-shots. Casper made the green in two, however, and then holed a long putt while Palmer was on in three, little more than a yard from the hole, but missed. Thereafter he fell steadily behind and reached his lowest ebb with a 7 on the long 16th.

How far, I wonder, did this unlikely failure erode Palmer's confidence? Remember at this time he was little more than a couple of years away from his last major championship victory, which was that complete domination of the 1964 US Masters. He was still only 36 and 'competitively young', having been a professional for very much the same number of years as, say, Seve Ballesteros today.

On the US Tour, however, he continued to be a major force until 1971, when he won four events and finished third in the money list. Perhaps it wasn't really until after the mid-1970s that Palmer really seemed a spent force. By then, he had despaired of his putting for many years. Perhaps oddly, he usually kept to his knock-kneed style and bothered most about whether he was keeping his head still. His collection of putters increased apace, which is always a sign of lost confidence. He no longer struck the ball firmly at the hole, knowing he could get the 3- or 4-footer back. Instead, he was far more defensive, dribbling the ball along so that he could at least be sure of a short tap-in to follow.

Yet the Arnold Palmer story is still a triumphant one, flawed only because his reign as a winner of major championships was shorter than we are entitled to expect. Yet he changed the face of golf by the bravura of his play. When he joined the US Tour, they were playing for total prize money of about $750,000. Today that figure is well over $20 million. Of course, inflation has a lot to do with it but US Tour players are chiefly indebted to Arnold Palmer. Although spectators might have been awed by the precision of Hogan or the swing of Snead, Palmer brought excitement to golf and the TV ratings for golf soared. In tournaments, though many might have followed their own favourites, Palmer always had his 'Army' and still has today. In the States, he made the greatest contribution to the popularizing of golf since Walter Hagen; elsewhere, he made the British Open the world's premier championship. You could make an epitaph out of that. He is the most exciting player I've ever seen.

PALMER, ARNOLD DANIEL
Born: Latrobe, Pennsylvania, USA, 10 September 1929
Major championship victories: 1954 US Amateur Championship;
1958 US Masters; 1960 US Masters, US Open Championship; 1961
British Open Championship; 1962 US Masters, British Open
Championship; 1964 US Masters.
Ryder Cup player: 1961, 1963, 1965, 1967, 1971, 1973
US Tour victories (1955–73): 61
Overseas victories (1961–75): 19
US Tour money winnings (1955–84): $1,887,693
World career money winnings (1955–84): $2,813,405

GARY
PLAYER

I can never decide which of my Supreme Champions I admire the most. If dedication, tenacity and making the most of natural ability are the yardsticks, there could hardly be two better candidates than Ben Hogan and Gary Player. Surely no one worked harder at improving their golf than these two.

When Gary first began to compete in British tournaments in the early 1950s, his talent looked limited indeed. I, for one, thought that more than anything else he lacked 'feel' for the game and I do think this is still evident today. Player doesn't make the little shots of golf look natural. Take his putting, for example, he seems to me to lock himself into a rigid stance and the stroke itself is a jab. His chipping is similar. There is not the delicate flow to his stroke that you can see in so many other good golfers. Instead, he strikes down at the ball and his clubhead follows into the turf and comes to an abrupt stop. Although his bunker stroke is naturally a much fuller one, Player adopts a variety of techniques from different types of sand, but his basic stroke buries the club firmly in the sand. He doesn't

No man has put more effort or thought into his shot-making than Gary Player. The US Open at Merion in 1981

often use the more usual method of sliding the clubhead under the ball, varying the depth depending on the length of shot needed or the consistency of the sand.

In each of these cases, however, time and the accumulation of titles have shown that Player is in the very highest class. His methods work. However, it wasn't Gary's short game which I and many of my fellow tournament golfers distrusted those many years ago but his basic swing. His grip was truly appalling with the right hand well under the shaft and four knuckles showing on the left hand. It resulted in an ugly flat swing and a huge hook. Gary, however, soon realized that his grip was faulty, learning particularly from that fine Welsh player, the late Dai Rees, who was one of the most consistent drivers ever. He moved his right hand over and set his left hand so that just two knuckles showed. Alas, that gave him a slice with some loss of distance but a few thousand practice balls later, Player arrived at a good compromise. The Vs between thumb and forefinger of both hands pointed towards his right eye, giving him a gain of some 30 to 40 yards from the tee. Even so, for a year or two more, his swing was still too flat and his stance too wide. He retained his hooker's hand action in the hitting area, the right hand tending to turn over too soon and close the blade of the club at impact.

Player had yet another serious problem which made us shake our wise heads: balance. Even at club level, you hardly ever see a good player off balance in the full swing except possibly at the end of the follow-through when striving for absolutely maximum distance. Young Gary most certainly didn't have good balance and that's usually death to consistent golf. He still isn't fully poised today which is perhaps the reason why he usually seems to try to lock his set-up into rigid positions.

Always one to seek advice, way back in 1956 Gary was apt to ask what his long-term career prospects were. Most thought them slim or none. Really, he should go back to South Africa, find another line of work and just play golf for fun. How wrong we were and how important determination and a passion to win are. Even more surprisingly, success for Player came very quickly. He turned professional at the age of 18 in 1953. In his first full attempt on the rather limited South African Tour of the early 1950s he had one second-place finish and at the end of the season was in the top 12. In 1955 he won his first tournament, the East Rand Open. With that, wider horizons beckoned. Then, as now, any South African golfer with ambitions must travel and Europe, perhaps, is the first continent to test their mettle. En route, he won his first international tournament, the Egyptian Matchplay Championship at the Gezira club outside Cairo. Although hardly a major event, it used to attract a field of good quality and winning is always important, particularly for a young golfer.

In view of what I said earlier, you might expect Gary's first few seasons overseas to have been disastrous. Yet, despite all his short-comings at the

His first win in Britain at Sunningdale in 1956 at the Dunlop tournament

time, they weren't. He won the Dunlop Tournament at Sunningdale, playing over 90 holes, which was a searching test indeed. The following year, he was brave enough to try the US Tour. From his home near Johannesburg, it was a daunting 46 hours' flying time to get there. Although by no means an overnight success, he probably covered his expenses and took a considerable step forward in 1958 when he won the Kentucky Open. Just as importantly, perhaps, he showed his worth in a major championship, finishing outright second in the US Open behind Tommy Bolt.

His first major championship victory wasn't far away and came at Muirfield in 1959. Player had already proved his ability in this event. In 1956 he was fourth and in 1958 seventh, which are results as good as many have to show for their efforts after a lifetime of trying. At Muirfield, Player was four behind the lead after three rounds and in contention only because he'd produced a very good second nine of 33, had gone to the turn in 34 and kept that momentum going with three birdies in the last nine. He faced the very difficult last hole needing a par-4 for a 66 and a total of 282, which would have needed inspired play from those still out on the course if they were to catch him.

Gary then bunkered his drive and later three-putted to take a two-over-par 6. For the 23-year-old, disappointment was bitter. He wept while his wife, Vivienne, tried to console him. Yet, as events were to show, the day wasn't lost. After all, his 68 had still set a stiff target. Those behind him with a real chance had to score between 70 and 72. One by one they fell away. The low rounds came from those who had started out without a chance of winning. Gary was champion after all and many rungs up the golfing ladder. He was on his way to becoming one of the leading figures in world golf.

However, in a sense, he had not won authoritatively. His victory was the result of others' failings and was a theme, as we shall see, which was to be repeated in his winning of major championships. For the time being, the world of golf remained unconvinced, not believing that another South African had arrived, soon to take over from Bobby Locke.

Gary Player was born the third child of Harry Audley Player, a gold mine captain and a 2 handicap golfer. His mother died when Gary was eight and his elder brother Ian, eight years his senior, was to be a strong influence, teaching Gary how to climb, box, lift weights and do plenty of physical training. Even more importantly, perhaps, he helped sharpen Gary's competitive instincts. At school, Gary proved to be an all-round athlete and he claims to have parred the first three holes of golf he ever played. By the age of 14 he was practising most of the daylight hours. As he was later to say: 'The more I practise, the luckier I get.'

Gary's dedication was by no means unusual for a young golfer. He was to prove much rarer in maintaining a punishing routine as year succeeded year. He gave very marked attention to the short game. At only 5 feet 8 inches, he could hardly hope to be a power hitter but precision on and around the green could, he thought, be an equalizer. He made a study of bunker play. After all, he would often be hitting longer clubs into greens than many of his future rivals, which made finding sand more likely. Player set himself goals. One of these was that he would continue practising from sand until he had *holed* five shots. He also spent hours chipping and putting, setting himself similar targets.

As regards long hitting, Player felt he had a different kind of answer. He'd make himself stronger and fitter than the rest. In this he was a true revolutionary, obvious though that may sound. When Gary grew up as a golfer there were few who put the fitness and body strength of an athlete high up on a list of the attributes a golfer most needs. Strong hands and good legs were obviously necessary but are developed well enough just by playing golf. The majority of professional golfers do little more today, though they look fitter. There are many who go for a run before breakfast and some who think off-season weight training useful and have a small gym at home. Even so, for many this is no more than a passing phase. If their golf improves they'll keep at it but otherwise decide that they are spoiling their swing by producing the wrong kind of muscles in the wrong places. Powerful shoulders, for example, have little influence in developing high clubhead speed.

Gary's fitness routines have varied over the years but he's basically concentrated on arm, hand, stomach and leg strength. He'll do 30 deep knee bends standing on each leg and 75 finger-tip push-ups just for starters. He also likes to stand on his head, which he believes promotes alertness, and takes two baths, one hot, one cold, to improve his circulation.

Player's beliefs about food and drink have also been widely publicized over many years. It's hardly surprising that he avoids alcohol and tobacco, perhaps thinking them the inventions of the devil, but he is almost equally opposed to coffee and tea. 'One day,' he's apt to say, 'the truth will come out about how bad those stimulants are for you.' He also avoids white bread, potatoes, fried foods, sugar and rich food in general. Instead, he's extolled the virtues of wheat germ, raw oats, fruit and vegetable juices, nuts, dried and fresh fruit and fish.

After the body, what about the mind? Here Gary is a disciple of Norman Vincent Peale, believing in the power of positive thinking. Convince yourself, Gary would say, that the course is in magnificent condition and you are at peak form and you have the right attitude to do battle in a tournament. Adopt the same frame of mind for each shot. See the flight of the ball and it pitching and running to your target. In essence, convince yourself that your every shot is going to be a good one and success will be the outcome.

At times, Gary has even believed that clothing is important. Of course, many golfers have adopted a personal trademark to make themselves more or less instantly recognizable: Locke's plus fours, Hogan's cap, the slicked-down hair of a Hagen or Cotton and Sam Snead's straw hat are all clear examples. Gary Player's trademark was an all-black outfit. In his case, however, there were practical reasons. Black absorbs sunlight and, Gary felt, helped both to keep him warm and to give him strength.

After his early swing troubles, Player made change after change so he's very much a manufactured golfer. For years now, his grip has been entirely conventional with left thumb straight down the shaft and the V of the right hand pointing between right shoulder and chin. At address, his posture seems rigid. He reaches for the ball, which is set well away from him, like Seve Ballesteros, and firms up every muscle in anticipation of the explosive effort to come. Gary then takes the club away low, keeping it close to the ground, as if intending to stretch every muscle. His total backswing is long, well past the horizontal and is achieved by a very full wrist cock, big shoulder turn but restricted hip pivot. He keeps his left arm exceptionally straight. It all means that he develops a swing arc comparable to many a man a foot taller. Player then hits as hard as he can!

With his first British Open under his belt, Player wanted more major championships. As ambitious as he is competitive, Player has always wanted to be known as the greatest golfer in the world. In 1957 he played his first US Masters but his first really good performance came in 1960 when he finished in joint sixth place, ironically with Ben Hogan, a man he admired above all others and who had advised him on his grip problems. But there had been another obstacle to success at Augusta. Gary didn't have enough length to make attempting to hit the par-5s in two sensible, with water in front to be carried. So off he went to develop more strength and flexibility. In 1960 at Augusta he had found the extra length and went into the lead after two rounds with scores of 69 and 68, tied with Arnold Palmer, holder of the Green Jacket.

On the third day, Player produced another sub-par round, a 69, which gave him a four-stroke advantage on the American. In the fourth round, Palmer began to charge from behind, as only he could, and there were errors from Gary. As he played the final hole, all seemed lost, for Palmer had gained five strokes to lead by one. Gary bunkered his second shot to the right of the green but managed get down in two more. Immediately behind, Palmer drove well but then lost his concentration. He'd made his charge, caught up and gone to the top of the leader board yet was about to throw away one of several major championships. His second shot drifted right into the same bunker and a play-off seemed likely unless he

Player drives: Palmer watches. This is 1964 when Player was one of the 'Big Three' with Palmer and Nicklaus

could match the South African's recent 'up and down' from sand. Instead, he took four more strokes to get down. Player became the first man from overseas to be Masters Champion. The gods had smiled on Player for the second time.

The following year, he won the US PGA and had now only one major championship barring his way to becoming one of only four golfers to win the Grand Slam of each of the major championships. This was the US Open. In 1965 the championship was held at Bellerive Country Club in Missouri. The course, though long at 7,191 yards, favoured Player's straight if not massive hitting for the Bermuda rough was long and tenacious. Very good putting would also be needed for the greens were both very large and lightning fast. Player began with two rounds of 70, which gave him a lead of one stroke over the Australian winner of the 1960 British Open, Kel Nagle, and the American Mason Rudolph. After a steady round of 71, with just one birdie in it, Player had increased his lead to two strokes over Nagle, while Rudolph had fallen away.

All week, Player had been reading *The Power of Positive Thinking* and concentrating on the single-minded notion of winning. In these thoughts he was even helped by a vision of sorts. He saw his name inscribed in gold on an honours board of US Open champions, next to that of Ken Venturi, winner the previous year at the Congressional club. Perhaps that win of Venturi's was in itself an inspiration. This American had come back to form after about two years at the very bottom and had then come through to win despite suffering heat exhaustion to the extent he needed a doctor to accompany him on his final round.

On the last day at Bellerive, Player had increased his lead to three strokes with fifteen holes played but at the 16th he was bunkered and dropped two strokes to par on the hole. Ahead, Nagle destroyed Gary's lead with a birdie on the 17th. How quickly things can change in golf. They ended tied with totals of 282. It meant that an overseas golfer would win the US Open for the first time since Englishman Ted Ray's victory back in 1920. In the play-off, Gary had one piece of 'luck'. A Nagle drive struck a lady spectator, cutting her quite badly. Nagle was extremely upset and his concentration was affected for some time. Perhaps it cost him the championship, perhaps not. Nevertheless, Player's score of 71 was good enough. Had the gods smiled again?

This victory gave him the Grand Slam, having won all four major championships, a feat which has not been achieved by most of my Supreme Champions – only Sarazen, Hogan and Nicklaus have done it to this day. The win removed all doubts of Gary's abilities. As we have seen earlier, contemporary professionals had had strong doubts; Flory van Donck, that beautiful Belgian player, said that Player would never win the British Open because his swing was too flat. It made Gary the more determined to prove him wrong. Even in South Africa it took time before he became an accepted sporting hero. Player once said: 'They said to my face and behind my back that I would never make a golfer. They are more responsible for my success than any other factor. By not believing in me they made me determined to prove them wrong.'

In South African golf, Player's success was amazing. Those who thought he'd never equal Bobby Locke's achievements on home ground can look at a record which included thirteen victories in the South African Open to Locke's nine. He has also won the South African PGA three times and the Masters ten. (It should, of course, be remembered that war cut a few years from Locke's career.) Outside his own country, Gary has proved to be the most successful international golfer of all time, winning on every continent, sometimes in events only a little below major championship status. There are seven Australian Open titles on his record and five World Matchplay Championships. On the US Tour he has had 21 victories, outstanding for a man who never played in the States full time.

Only a man of Player's enormous drive could have achieved even half of this. With very few exceptions, professional golfers are happiest and at their best when playing on their home tour where at least the faces of fellow players, administrators and the Press are familiar. Most Americans who have passed the qualifying school for the US Tour stay strictly at home, venturing abroad only if they are among the elite and then for very brief periods – perhaps to play the British or Australian Opens and the occasional other tournament if the appearance money is good enough. Europeans are a little more adventurous and appear, for example, in Africa, on the Asian Circuit and in Australia, but only in the off-season. The Japanese are even less daring. Their home tour is very lucrative and only a handful ever compete outside the Far East. But watch out for them. Their stature grows yearly and the Spaniards' and Swedes' also. The South Africans and the Australians are the true world travellers, mainly because their competitive seasons are short and there's no large fortune to be made from prize money on their home grounds. Among these travellers, however, Gary Player has covered far more miles than anyone else in his desire to be the greatest golfer of all time.

Gary didn't continue to amass major championships year after year in the style of a Nicklaus, Hogan or Jones and was perhaps not quite of the same calibre. I don't think he had the ability to raise his game for the biggest events to the extent just a few others have been able to do. However, in one of the longest careers of all as a top golfer, he kept plugging away, never giving up, and victories continued to come his way from time to time. One of his dearest ambitions was to win another US Open so that, like Jack Nicklaus, he could complete the Grand Slam of the four major championships twice. In that, he hasn't succeeded and is unlikely to do so now even if his tie for second place in the 1984 US PGA Championship, which included a round of 63, was considered one of the greatest achievements by an 'old' golfer. (Player was approaching his forty-ninth birthday at the time.)

After that 1965 US Open, Gary was established as one of the so-called 'Big Three' of world golf, together with Palmer and Nicklaus. The money flowed in and his schedule of world travel was hectic as he piled up tournament victory on victory. At home, he owned a ranch some 250 miles from Johannesburg in the Magoebaskloof Mountains which he named Bellerive in commemoration of his US Open victory. There he kept about 100 horses, 35 stables and there was even a race track. Elsewhere, Player has specialized in growing flowers and has a home, Zonnehoeve Plaas, at a convenient commuting distance from Johannesburg. He has, one might say, rejoiced in the fruits of his victories with both ostentation and style, pursuing a passionate interest in the breeding of thoroughbred horses. He loves to attend the Newmarket sales when he is in Britain.

Very early in his career, he married Vivienne Verwey, whom he'd met when she worked in her father's pro shop. They have six children, two boys and four girls, and all have been brought up in a highly-competitive sporting atmosphere, just as Gary himself was. Someone once said that the prime cause of Gary's success was that 'He likes beating people' and sometimes it seems as if he also enjoys beating his children as well. It's said that, whatever the sport or activity, Gary goes all out to win.

In 1968 Player won his second British Open. The setting was Carnoustie on the east coast of Scotland; the principal opponent, Jack Nicklaus. It didn't look like this after the first round, however. Player's 74 was four strokes behind the leaders, the amateur Michael Bonallack and Brian Barnes, the latter of whom, in those far-off days, looked a very likely future Open Championship winner. The next day, Billy Casper moved ahead, his rounds of 72 and 68 giving him a lead of five strokes on Gary. Jack Nicklaus, after an opening round of 76, followed with the second lowest round of the day, a 69. The third day, Player had the lowest score, a 71, though a few others equalled it. Casper's lead was cut to a single stroke and he was joined as front-runner by the New Zealander Bob Charles, the only left-hander ever to win a major championship. Then came the South African, with Jack Nicklaus two strokes further behind.

Both Charles and Casper quickly fell away and it looked odds on that the title would go to Player or Nicklaus. At the 6th, a par-5 he was looking to birdie, Nicklaus hooked out of bounds to fall three behind. He began going for his shots, seeking maximum distance from the tee and firing straight for the flag instead of opting for safer routes to the green. On the 13th, Nicklaus got a shot back and then birdied the 14th. But that birdie just wasn't good enough. Player flew a magnificent blind second shot over the Spectacles bunkers and his ball came to rest just a couple of feet from the hole. It was a truly great shot but of course there was that vital element of luck as well. His three-stroke lead restored, Player hung on to the end.

A similarly 'lucky' shot in the closing holes brought Player his next major championship, the 1972 US PGA. With rounds of 71, 71 and 67 he had a slender one-stroke lead over Billy Casper going into the final round.

Then he seemed to throw it all away with a start of bogey, birdie, bogey, bogey. As play continued at the very difficult Oakland Hills course, nearly a dozen golfers jockeyed for the lead. Player got in the decisive blow on the 16th. After slicing his drive, his ball lay in wet grass and there was some 150 yards, a tall tree and a water hazard between him and the hole. His shot with a 9-iron had to be a furious lash to get both height and the distance too. I would think it owed quite a lot to chance. His ball came to rest not much more than 3 feet from the hole. He got the putt. It was his sixth major championship.

His best year was still to come and was undoubtedly 1974. In April, he won his second US Masters. Four strokes off the lead after two rounds, Player then birdied five holes in a row from the 12th to the 16th and the 66 which followed brought him to within a stroke of the leader, the solid and tough Dave Stockton. The final round was a very close run thing. With the final nine still to play, any one of at least eight golfers were very possible winners. Gary produced his killer blow on the 17th, hitting his approach shot to within inches of the hole. No luck this time. It was a perfect golf shot.

After winning the Memphis Classic not long after, luck again had little to do with a real triumph in the British Open at Royal Lytham. The American-size ball was compulsory for the first time and in the stiff winds

A poised finish to the swing this time: Player in action at Augusta National

many could not control it. Gary relied heavily on his 1-iron to hold the fairways and keep his ball under the wind and, looking back on it, was not severely pressed throughout. He had arrived with what he called his 'new swing'. The one he'd been winning with for nearly 20 years had been no good at all. His opening 69 was good enough to share the first-round lead and the 68 which followed put him well ahead – by five strokes in fact, the largest margin at that stage since Henry Cotton 40 years before. The next best score was a 70. In the third round, however, Gary's 75 gave his pursuers a glimmer of hope. Even so, he still led Peter Oosterhuis by two and Nicklaus by three. The rest of the field seemed out of touch – and so it was to prove. With a mixture of birdies, bogeys and an eagle, Player reached the turn in 32 and with a birdie on the 10th was six strokes in the lead. Even so there was trouble ahead. On the 17th, Player pulled his second shot way left of the green. His ball was only something like 20 yards from the flag but in long and thick rough. Player took his time reaching his ball to give the stewards time to look. He pulled out his watch when he reached the scene to time the five minutes he was allowed and led the search parties ever more energetically as the minutes passed. The ball was found, almost on the time limit, and Player hacked it out to the fringe before getting down in two more strokes for a one-over-par-5. The championship was his and the final problem no more than a happening of interest. He put his second shot through the last green, hard by the clubhouse wall and, you could say, became the first golfer since Bob Charles to play his final shot to the green left-handed, with that trusty black-headed putter, so long his favourite.

Towards the end of the year Gary made the record books again as the first golfer to break 60 in a national championship, the Brazilian Open. This is what his round looked like: 3, 4, 3, 3, 4, 2, 3, 3, 4; 2, 4, 3, 4, 4, 4, 2, 4, 3. 29 out, 30 in. He was the unrivalled golfer of the year.

Player was by this time into his forties. His earnings in the States began to fall away but he still had a very good year left, really a superb three weeks in April 1978. Happily for him, it began in a major championship, the Masters, of course. After three rounds of 72, 72, 69, he was seven strokes behind the leader, Hubert Green. With eight holes played in the final round, little had changed. But at this point the birdies began to flow. The crowds appeared little interested in Player. Attention was focused on Tom Watson, Hubert Green and Rod Funseth, the trio who surely would provide the champion. Gary was irritated and turned to his partner, Ballesteros: 'Seve, I want to tell you something. Those people don't think I can win. You watch. I'll show them.' That 'I'll show them' has been a motivating force for Gary throughout his career and Seve Ballesteros says: 'Player likes to think people are against him so he can fight harder'.

He certainly fought hard that day, birdied seven, yes seven, of the last ten holes and came in with a 64 which equalled the Masters record. Even

Player with his caddie 'Rabbit' Dyer during the 1984 US PGA Championship at Shoal Creek in which he tied for second place with Lanny Wadkins, four strokes behind Lee Trevino

so, perhaps he still shouldn't have won. Tom Watson, for instance, missed the green rather wildly to the left on the last hole and dropped a shot, which left him one stroke behind Gary and Hubert Green missed a putt of no more than 3 feet to tie. It was Player's third Masters' title. The gods were yet again smiling.

The victory qualified him to compete in the Tournament of Champions the following week. Again he began the final round seven strokes behind the leader, which he might have felt was quite a good omen, especially as Ballesteros was once again on hand. Seve, however, had a 79 in the final round and Player a 67, easily the best of the day. Another win.

Onwards to Houston. Here Player again saw reflections of the Masters, this time beginning rather than ending with a 64 but, after rounds of 67 and 70 to follow he contrived to go into the last round three behind and with a round of 69 beat Andy Bean by a stroke. He became the eleventh man to win three events in a row on the US Tour. Could he make it four? This time Gary changed the script. He began with rounds of 69, 67 and

69 to share the lead in the New Orleans Open. His last round 72 was no match for a 66 from Lon Hinkle and the spell was broken.

On 1 November 1985, Gary Jim Player was 50 years old and now qualifies for the US Seniors Tour and the challenge of showing them he's the fittest and best 50-year-old golfer in the world. I expect the gods will still be on his side.

PLAYER, GARY JIM
Born: Johannesburg, South Africa, 1 November 1935
Major championship victories: 1959 British Open Championship;
1961 US Masters; 1962 US PGA Championship; 1965 US Open
Championship; 1968 British Open Championship; 1972 US PGA
Championship; 1974 US Masters, British Open Championship;
1978 US Masters.
US Tour victories (1958–78): 21
Total career victories (1955–84): 128
US Tour money winnings (1957–84): $1,784,962
European Tour money winnings (1955–84): £160,267
World career money winnings (1955–84): $3,100,881

JACK
NICKLAUS

When a young man turns tournament professional, the trumpets are often muted. Very often he will have shown considerable promise and there may be a few trophies on the mantelpiece but they will almost certainly come from amateur events the golfing public care little if anything about today. The knowing ones may have noted his ability but even national amateur champions and Walker Cup team members as often as not quickly disappear in the heat of professional competition. Flaws of both technique and personality quickly find them out.

In the case of Jack Nicklaus, however, it was all very different. Indeed, he is the last great player to have seriously considered remaining an amateur. Nicklaus, from as early as his teens, had always wanted to become the greatest golfer the world had ever seen. His idol was Bobby Jones. 'Could I,' he wondered, 'be greater than he was and also remain an amateur?' For a little while, money considerations were secondary. He came from a reasonably prosperous family and was selling insurance – not too difficult if you're a top amateur golfer and mixing with the rich and famous at the country clubs and great courses of the United States.

Eventually, Jack made the decision to turn professional, primarily because he felt that the best competition was on the US Tour. It was there he must test himself. By that time, he had the most brilliant record, at least in the short term, of anyone of modern times in amateur golf and had also amply proved he could compete at the highest levels of professional golf.

Jack Nicklaus began playing golf at the age of ten and was always encouraged by his father, Charlie, whom Jack has described as his best friend. The family came from Alsace-Lorraine, that region which has alternated between being French and German. Nicklaus's great-grandfather made a start to founding the family fortunes in the States by establishing a boiler works in Columbus, Ohio, the city where Jack himself was to grow up as the elder of two children. His father owned a pharmacy and, by the time Jack was a young man of twenty, owned four.

As well as his father's encouragement, Jack also benefited from having the same golf coach right from the beginning. He was, and still is, Jack Grout, himself no mean golfer who had enjoyed some success in tournament play. The young Nicklaus's progress was rapid indeed. After taking something like 150 for his first round of golf, he was able to score an 81 about a year later. Breaking 80 is one of the milestones of golf and Jack, too, found it a barrier. At the age of 12, he did it with sudden ease – a round of 74. Seldom again did he score in the 80s!

Already some of the trademarks of the way Jack Nicklaus plays had been established. From his father, he picked up the interlocking grip while Grout encouraged him to develop as big a swing arc as possible and to hit hard. Grout felt that control can be added later, while smooth swingers often lose their game if they try to add more punch and clubhead speed in their efforts to add length to their game.

In competitive golf, Jack followed no different a path from other young club golfers. First there were successes at club and local level and at 15 he won the Columbus amateur titles at both junior and senior levels. The following year he was playing state and national golf. He won the Ohio Junior title and, a big step forward, the state's Open. He also reached the semi-final of the US Junior Championship. When 17 he qualified to play in the US Open and two rounds of 80, over a course set up at its most testing for the championship, were no disgrace.

By the end of the 1950s, Jack Nicklaus was one of the country's leading amateurs. He became his country's amateur champion in 1959, beating Charles Coe by one up in a magnificent final. Coe was a player good enough to have finished sixth in the US Masters that same year and was to finish only a stroke behind the champion a couple of years later.

You can sense the brutal power of young Jack Nicklaus

The same year, Nicklaus played in the Walker Cup over a course which was to feature much in his future career – Muirfield. He won both his foursomes and singles matches. He also made his début on the US Tour and finished twelfth in a tournament after opening rounds of 67 and 66. However, the feats that stamped him as a golfer of almost unlimited prospects still lay ahead – but not very far. The US Open at Cherry Hills in 1960 saw both the rise to superstar status of Arnold Palmer and Ben Hogan's last real run at the title. Playing with Hogan was the young Jack Nicklaus, who began with rounds of 71, 71 and 69, which gave him a four-stroke lead on Arnold. However, Palmer's record-breaking 65 wasn't to be denied. He was the year's champion and Jack was outright second, just two strokes behind, after a closing round of 71.

Good though this was, his totally dominant performance in the World Amateur Team Championship for the Eisenhower Trophy has never been

Still 'fat', Jack. Jack Nicklaus on his first professional appearance in Britain at Hillside Golf Club in Lancashire in 1962, which was not a happy time

approached in quality. He finished at eleven under par on 269 after rounds of 66, 67, 68 and 68. There were those who pointed out that Ben Hogan had taken 18 strokes more when he won the US Open over the same course, Merion, nearly 20 years earlier. When he was to write about this performance several years later, Jack considered it, despite a few major championships under his belt since, the best golf he had ever played. If so, he had reached a peak at the age of 20 and, as an amateur, had proved all the points.

A year later, Jack turned professional. In the meantime he had made his second Walker Cup appearance and won both the NCAA Championship and the US Amateur once more. No one, of course, was in any doubt at all that he'd be a great success in professional golf. The question was: How soon? He won money on his first US Tour professional appearance at the Los Angeles Open, a modest $33. Soon larger cheques began to come in and before long he had a second-place finish in the Phoenix Open.

For his first win, Nicklaus chose the best event of all, the US Open, and the main opponent was right also – Arnold Palmer, who led Nicklaus by two with a round to go. However, Jack's final round of 69 was good enough to tie him with the year's Masters champion and a play-off over 18 holes followed the next day. There were no signs of youthful nerves in Nicklaus's start the following day. After six holes, he held a four-stroke lead over Palmer. Although Palmer fought back, the margin was much the same at the end: Nicklaus 71; Palmer 74.

It was by no means a popular victory. Palmer was the American hero, the most charismatic golfer since Bobby Jones and just as well liked. The young Jack Nicklaus was not. For a start, he was upsetting Palmer's apple cart and even if American crowds always flock to a winner they didn't like what they saw when they looked at Jack Nicklaus. He was unsmiling, overweight and certainly didn't dress the part. Jack paid little if any attention to what the well-dressed golfer was wearing and was apt to play throughout a tournament in the same pair of slacks and a jockey cap with the peak turned up, concealing his crew-cut hairdo. The pace of his play also won him no friends. Although he walked briskly enough between shots, he seemed to set himself over the ball for an age, on every shot he played.

Of course, Jack was aware of all the criticism but did little about it during his early years as a professional. The main reason was that he just didn't care. His aim was tunnel-visioned on being the greatest golfer the world had ever seen. That had little to do with colour-coordinated golf outfits and charm. As he once remarked: 'You have to bear down and get that ball into the cup. Any jerk can miss it gracefully.' Already, he was at his best at 'bearing down' in the major championships. In 1963, two more came his way, his first Masters and the PGA. In the Masters, he was five strokes behind the leaders after a first-round 74 but was firmly in contention after a brilliant 66 on the second day. In a generally high-scoring championship, with the lead fluctuating on the final day, he won his first green jacket by a single stroke from Tony Lema.

In the US PGA, Nicklaus had been third on his first appearance the previous year but his victory at Dallas Athletic Country Club put him, in only his second year of professional golf, into a very select group indeed. At the time, only Gene Sarazen, Ben Hogan and Byron Nelson had won the US Open, Masters and PGA in their careers – that's how rare major championship victories are. Even by this time, Nicklaus's prime goal was to win a major championship every year. In this sense, 1964 was something of a disappointment. He didn't win one and had to make do with just a quartet of US Tour events and the position of leading money winner for the first time.

After his first season as a professional, Jack knew that the money would always roll in if he continued to be a great player, but perhaps this is the time to reflect on his achievements as a money winner, despite the fact that he never came close to playing all the events and soon learned to limit his tournament appearances to keep his competitive edge as keen as possible. From 1962 to the end of 1978, he never finished a US Tour season out of the top four, a span of time no one has come remotely near equalling. If we go a little further, the record then reveals that Nicklaus was as bad as fourth only twice. In the other years he was first eight times, second five times and third the rest.

By the end of 1984, his US Tour winnings alone totalled more than $4½ million with Tom Watson, aided by the much higher prize money every year, a million dollars behind but still his closest rival.

In 1965 Nicklaus produced one of his greatest performances in a major championship. The setting was Augusta National and the event, of course, was the US Masters. After an opening round of 67, he was two strokes behind Gary Player but was tied with the South African and Arnold Palmer after the second day. Nicklaus then produced what I consider the greatest round ever played at Augusta. I'm not talking just about the score, which was a 64, but rather the way it was compiled.

He had eight birdies and ten pars, missed only two fairways and was on the green with his first or second shot except on the par-4 17th, where his shot spun back just off the green. Thirty putts were used and there wasn't a 5 on his card.

At this time, Nicklaus was hitting his maximum length, which was about 300 yards and it's interesting to look at what clubs he used from tee to green. Remember at Augusta there is never excessive run on the ball. This can happen from time to time, for instance, on a British links course during a dry summer, when the Jack Nicklaus of the 1960s might find himself debating between a sand-iron or a soft-wedge on a par-5. With the dense turf and watered fairways at Augusta you get what you hit. At every hole, except, of course, the par-3s, Jack used his driver first and then needed the following:

Hole	Yards	Club	Hole	Yards	Club
1	400	sand-iron	10	485	8-iron
2	555	3-iron and wedge	11	445	8-iron
3	355	wedge	12	155	8-iron
4	220	4-iron	13	475	5-iron
5	450	6-iron	14	420	7-iron
6	190	6-iron	15	520	5-iron
7	365	wedge	16	190	6-iron
8	530	3-iron	17	400	8-iron
9	420	wedge	18	420	wedge

At the end of the day, the field trailed far behind and remained there when Jack scored a 69 in the last round. His total for the championship was 271 and he had won by nine strokes. Both his third round and total remain a record, though there have been scores to equal both before and since. His winning margin, however, remains a Masters record. It prompted Bobby Jones, who had watched him play, to remark: 'Jack is playing an entirely different game, a game I'm not even familiar with.' He didn't, though, let himself be drawn too far into evaluating the historical status of Jack Nicklaus. Jones was well aware of the vast differences in equipment and course conditions from one era to another. Jones himself had had a far better time of it than the first great players who had had to cope with courses where bunkers were not raked, fairways and greens rough cut and the rest left to grow wild. He too played with hickory shafts but, in his retirement from competitive play, immediately adopted steel shafts once they became available. He contented himself with saying: 'It is safe to say that there has not been a more effective golfer than Jack Nicklaus.'

'Effective' was indeed very much the right word for Nicklaus in his early twenties. Later, he was to admit that his basic approach was to overpower a golf course. He set out to hit his tee-shot a very long way, find the ball and then fire it at the green. He knew that length made things a great deal easier. The green is a lot easier target with a wedge from even quite clinging rough than a 4-iron from centre fairway. If Jack missed a green, he was by no means a master at getting the ball to the holeside once he wasn't playing a full shot. He lacked feel for the short game, except when putting. As he later said: 'I used to just slop it on the green and I knew I could make a lot of the putts.'

This attitude was to change with the passing of the years and, as I hope we'll see, Jack did develop his short game though he never approached the flair of a Ballesteros or Johnny Revolta. Even more importantly, he thought more and more about how to play a particular course and how to win.

In 1966 he became the first man to defend a Masters title successfully. This time, it was a much closer-fought affair and Jack had to come through a three-way play-off over 18 holes. Unlike Gary Player, however, he had yet to win each of the major titles. The British Open had eluded him in his first four attempts. In 1962, newly crowned as US Open Champion, he had floundered well down the field, only just qualifying to play the final 36 holes. 'Ah yes,' they said, 'this fellow Nicklaus can't play links golf. He hits the ball too high to play well in the wind and is used to hitting to well-watered greens. He'll really have to learn the old Scottish pitch and run shot – if he can.'

However, that first year he was playing Troon in fiendish conditions. The course was hard and bouncy and, as I say elsewhere, only Palmer and Kel Nagle found the answers. The next year, 1963, Nicklaus almost pulled it off at Royal Lytham and St Anne's. After two rounds he lay third, three strokes behind the leader, Phil Rodgers of the USA, with the Australian Peter Thomson in between. On the final morning, New Zealander Bob Charles was round in 66 and led the field with Thomson one behind, followed by Nicklaus and Rodgers with two strokes to make up. No one else was in it. In the final round, Nicklaus made a typical move on the 553-yard 7th hole, covering the distance with a drive and 5-iron to 3 feet for an eagle 3. After ten holes he held the lead for the first time. He lost the championship by the narrowest of margins, a single stroke, over the closing holes. He three-putted the 15th but followed with a birdie on the next, before dropping shots on each of the last two holes, both a stern test. In the end, Charles and Rodgers holed shortish putts on the last hole to beat him and went into a play-off the next day, the New Zealander coming out on top by 140 to 148.

In 1964 at St Andrews Nicklaus was beaten by a better man that particular year – Tony Lema. Lema played splendidly throughout and thoroughly deserved the championship. Even so, there were signs for all to read. On the final day Nicklaus hauled himself up the field with rounds of 66 and 68. All through, his power had been awesome and he drove the last green, some 350 yards, as a matter of routine. Yet his putting had been hesitant until the last day, when he forced himself to trust his judgement of line on the short putts and went straight at the hole. His finish was magnificent – but it came too late. Lema was champion by five strokes and Nicklaus was second.

His time was soon to come, at Muirfield in 1966, which was a course he knew and liked from his Walker Cup experiences several years before. The course as set up, however, favoured the short, straight hitter. The rough had been allowed to grow in and the fairways were some of the narrowest I've seen in the driving area, some 250 yards from the tee. The R and A had followed the US Golf Association's lead by letting the rough grow in around the greens. That year, you couldn't miss a green and think you'd be down with a chip and a putt. The course rewarded those that didn't wander too far off the fairway and hit the greens.

Power play still benefited Nicklaus but mainly because of his length and control with the long-irons. He seldom used woods from the tee, just as so many players have learned to do in later years whenever faced with a course that imposes severe penalties on a drive that's good, but not good enough. After two rounds, Nicklaus led Peter Butler narrowly by one stroke but was two strokes behind Rodgers going into the final 18 holes. With four holes to go he needed level par to tie the Welshman David Thomas and Doug Sanders, in with scores of 283. He did better than that. His victory by a stroke put him in the company of Hogan, Sarazen and Player as men who have won each of the four major championships. But only Nicklaus was to complete the feat twice and, as if to emphasize superiority, made it three Grand Slams in the years ahead, a task he completed in the 1978 British Open at St Andrews.

Although Nicklaus will probably end his career with 'only' three British Opens on his record, this is the championship which has seen his most consistent performances. From 1963 to 1980 he had one twelfth placing, a sixth and a fifth. The rest of the time Jack was fourth or better, with seven second-place finishes, which is astounding. He has played in the championship 24 times and never failed to make both the 36- and 54-hole cuts, until 1985. Overall, in such a prolonged period, not even Vardon, Taylor and Braid were quite as consistent.

In 1967 Nicklaus failed to qualify in the US Masters after being first or second for the previous four years. He made full amends in the US Open at Baltusrol a couple of months later, winning the championship for the second time. With the final round still to play, Nicklaus was level with Arnold Palmer and the previous year's champion, Billy Casper. His 65 then gave him the championship by four strokes from Palmer and equalled the record for a champion's last round. His 275 total was a new US Open record, beating Hogan's mark set in 1948. It was to remain the record for a good many years – until broken by Jack himself.

Early in his professional career, as I said earlier, Nicklaus set himself the prime target of winning at least one of the four major championships every year – though preferably all of them! Judging by these high standards, his game fell away for the next three seasons. He averaged only two individual victories a season, none of which were major championships. It started to be asked if Nicklaus was beginning to weary of it all. Afterwards, he was to say: 'Golf is my love and my career but it never has been everything.' Was the motivation dwindling with nine major championships (including his two US Amateurs) won?

The answer came at St Andrews in 1970, when Nicklaus had managed nothing better than a sixth place in a major championship for two years. It was not an outstanding performance by Nicklaus and is remembered more for Doug Sanders's failure to par the last hole, one of the easiest 4s you could ever hope to meet, than for Nicklaus's win after an 18-hole play-off. But it set him on his way again.

The next half-a-dozen seasons saw Nicklaus at a new peak. He lost a little of his awesome power, a result of passing youth and a slimming

A very important
championship in a great
career. Nicklaus with his
wife Barbara after winning
the 1970 British Open

programme but was learning to increase his range of strokes. Nicklaus
was indeed cutting a more attractive figure on the golf course. He grew
his hair and had learned to smile. His outfits were colour-coordinated. He
was a glamour boy. Increasingly, as the unquestioned world number one
he saw himself as an ambassador for the game and there could hardly
have been a better one, modest in victory and rueful, not scowling, in
defeat.

From 1971 to 1976 he was five times leading money winner on the US
Tour and the major championships continued to come his way in a steady
flow. The year of 1972 was perhaps his best. On the US Tour he played
only 19 events, winning 7 of them and finishing in the top ten 14 times.
He won both the US Masters and Open by three strokes. The latter victory
was a milestone. It was his thirteenth major championship and equalled
Bobby Jones's record, which had stood for more than 40 years. Jones had
achieved the feat by the age of 28 and retired; Nicklaus was 32 and eager
for more.

In that same season, 1972, Nicklaus made his closest run at winning all four major championships in one year, with two under his belt when he arrived at Muirfield for the British Open. It was not to be – but how close he came. Jack went into the final round no fewer than six strokes behind the leader, Lee Trevino. So often a cautious player, unwilling to let others prosper because bold shots might get him into trouble, Nicklaus once again went for everything when there were no other options.

He reached the turn in 32 and then birdied both the 10th and the 11th – 11 holes in just 38 strokes was golf almost beyond belief. For a short while, he led the championship. However, on the remaining holes a birdie opportunity or two were missed and he dropped one shot. It was not quite good enough and Trevino, helped by a few outrageous bits of luck, took the title by a stroke. What drama there'd have been if Jack had done it. He'd have passed Jones's tally of championships and how the world of golf would have looked forward to 3 August 1972, the day the US PGA Championship began.

A year later at Canterbury, in his home state of Ohio, Nicklaus moved past Jones by taking his fourteenth major title, the US PGA, and with some ease as he was four strokes ahead at the finish. It could have been a time to consider retirement and Jack didn't have a particularly good season in 1974. However, 1975 was a very good year.

By the time the 1975 Masters came round, Nicklaus had already won two tournaments but for the first time for some years there was a challenger to his unquestioned supremacy, Johnny Miller. He had won eight US events in 1974, the most since Arnold Palmer in 1960 and had beaten Jack's money-winning record in doing so. He was in much the same mood early in 1975, with three more wins. Hindsight shows that Miller was soon to fade from his peak but at the time of the US Masters there were grounds for thinking that Johnny Miller just might turn out to be the greatest golfer ever. After all he was dominating the US Tour in a way not even Nicklaus had. Miller himself said: 'Happiness is knowing even your poor shots are still better than the next guy's good ones!'

Nicklaus put in a statement of intent with a formidable start – 68 – and then 67. He was five ahead of his closest challengers, Palmer and a new name, Tom Watson, with Tom Weiskopf a stroke further away. Miller, after an opening 75 followed by a 71, was nowhere.

All this was to change in the third round. Perhaps Nicklaus played a little too cautiously, while Miller and Weiskopf knew they had to go for everything. Miller's start was prodigious. After parring the 1st, he birdied the next six and reached the turn in 30. Both were records. Miller brought in a 65 and was now only three behind Jack. Weiskopf did just as well, his 66 taking him into a one-stroke lead for the championship. Weiskopf knew he could win; Nicklaus had to start all over again; Miller hoped to carry on his form of the day before. To the turn, Nicklaus took 35, Weiskopf 34 and Miller 32, which included five birdies. It was still anyone's championship but Weiskopf, two ahead of both Nicklaus and Miller, looked to have the best chance.

Nicklaus made no move for some time, parring the next four holes and then dropping a shot to par on the 14th but it was the 15th and 16th that settled the championship. They were played with Weiskopf still holding a one-stroke lead over Nicklaus, with Miller a stroke behind. For his second shot to this 520-yard hole over water, Nicklaus fired a 1-iron straight at the flag, the best one he'd hit, he later remarked, for several years. Weiskopf sent his second shot with a 4-iron just through the back of the green while Miller was well right of the flag with a 4-wood.

In the end each got his birdie but Tom Weiskopf's seemed the most significant because he had needed a 4-yard putt for it. With the 1973 British Open under his belt, surely another major was overdue? At the 16th, a par-3 of about 190 yards, Nicklaus hit no more than a moderate tee-shot. It was always well short of the flag and rolled back down the slope to leave him a putt of about 15 yards, a huge borrow all the way. It just wasn't on. Yet down it went and Jack leapt in the air for joy.

Minutes later, Tom Weiskopf lost the Masters at the same hole. His iron shot was hit even more heavily than Jack's and he three-putted. With a lead of one stroke, Jack parred the last two holes very securely, each time coasting his approach putts dead. Miller birdied the 17th to close the gap to a single stroke but neither Weiskopf nor Miller could prise a birdie at the last. Both finished a stroke behind Jack, who called it all: 'The most exciting day of golf I can remember in 15 years.' It was his fifth Masters title, a record, and his fifteenth major championship.

Another followed some four months later, his fourth PGA, where he was able to change a four-stroke deficit on the Australian Bruce Crampton after two rounds, which included a record 63 from Crampton, to win by two strokes. Although Nicklaus continued to win both large sums of money and occasional tournaments over the next three years, the flow of major championships was halted. All was not right with his game and he was increasingly aware that his short game just wasn't good enough. The competition was getting sharper all the time and scores were improving, mainly because there were more and more players capable of winning who had the short game talents that Nicklaus just didn't. One way of putting it would be to say he was no Tom Watson. Nicklaus himself found that he scored much the same on any course, whether it was a difficult or a relatively easy one. On the tough courses, the quality of his long game showed up as well as ever; on easier lay-outs he was not as good as many others at getting down in two when he missed a green.

Although he added the 1978 British Open to his record, giving him his third grand slam of the four major championships and his seventeenth championship success, a disastrous year lay just ahead. In the USA, his money winnings plummeted to just $59,434. Despite the huge increases in prize money, it was the least he had earned in his entire professional career. Worse, he stood seventy-first on the end of season money list, when fourth had been his lowest performance as a tournament player. His stroke average was about 1½ shots worse per round than the previous year. Perhaps the king's reign was over?

Looking back, I think we can see now that in a sense it was. Tom Watson and, soon, Seve Ballesteros were to overtake him as the most regular contenders for the major championships. Nicklaus was never again to be number one but there was no apparent reason why Jack should not continue to be one of the great players – if he cared enough. In 1979 it had seemed that perhaps he didn't. He competed in just 12 tournaments in the United States which was hardly enough to maintain his edge. But Nicklaus did care and decided to go back to school again.

Jack Grout told him that flaws had leaked into his long game and Nicklaus agreed. He had kept his high backlift but his arms weren't swinging to the rear as well as up. At the top he didn't feel properly coiled. His attack on the ball was too steep and lack of length became a problem, together with inconsistency. His divots were very much across the line and ran from right to left, a slicing action in fact.

For the short game, he consulted Phil Rodgers, an extraordinary putter who was prominent in at least two British Opens of the 1960s and who might have won either. Rodgers felt that Jack should take the wrists out of his chip shots and use something much nearer a putting action. On the little high shots, he counselled more hand action. Nicklaus practised as he hadn't in the off-season for years. Why, one might ask, did he bother at the age of 40? From Nicklaus himself comes the answer: 'My record wasn't yet quite the one I wanted to leave behind.'

He emerged feeling that, in the long game, he was getting the clubhead solidly into the back of the ball again and that he had a better understanding of his swing than ever before. His short game, he felt, was 'reasonable' and he'd have to settle for that. Nicklaus knew that he just wasn't gifted with touch but he had other talents, especially nerve, which was unimpaired.

In March he lost a play-off to Ray Floyd in the Doral-Eastern but that kind of revival wasn't maintained. In the US Masters, for instance, he was well down the field and then, a week before the US Open had the rare experience of missing the 36-hole cut in a tournament, the Atlanta Classic.

He chose the place for a return to form well – Baltusrol and the US Open. On the first day, both Nicklaus and Tom Weiskopf, with 63s, tied the US Open record. While Tom rapidly fell away with his other rounds in the mid-70s, Nicklaus capitalized on a start where he had missed a putt of about 2½ feet on the last green for a round of 62. His 71 in the second round was a far more tentative performance and, as in the third round, one had the feeling that Nicklaus was playing defensive golf. Someone a little down the field going for his shots might well catch him.

The greatest danger was the Japanese Isao Aoki, with whom Jack played throughout the championship. When Nicklaus missed an 8-foot putt on the 14th in his third round, Aoki drew up to just a stroke behind. Tom Watson, too, eight strokes behind after Nicklaus's 63, followed with rounds of 68 and 67. At the end of the third day he lay just two behind.

In the closing stages of Nicklaus's third round, he seemed to have feet of clay. There was a crisis, for instance, on the 15th when he left his approach putt several feet short and then knocked this putt about 3 feet past before holing the next. On the 16th, 216 yards, Jack was himself again with a superb long-iron which covered the flag, though he failed to birdie the hole. On the 17th, a monster par-5 of 630 yards, he hit a good drive but then topped his 3-wood club second shot, leaving himself about 175 yards to go with the ball well below his feet. This time his swing was as good as his previous one had been bad and he nearly birdied the hole. On the 18th, he allowed Aoki to catch him when he three-putted. Jack often seemed to first fall short with tentative putts and then over-compensate by being too strong.

It was a different Nicklaus who emerged on the final day. He decided to play aggressively, with Aoki level, Lon Hinkle only a stroke behind and the trio of Tom Watson, Mark Hayes and Keith Fergus two off the lead. Nicklaus's driving was excellent throughout, his air of composure complete and his putting always sound. He ended in fine style with putts for birdies on the last two holes. His 272 total was a new US Open record and gave him a two-stroke margin over Aoki. It was his eighteenth major championship and he became one of only nine to lead the US Open from start to finish. His fourth victory in the event is also a record, which he shares with Ben Hogan, Willie Anderson and Bobby Jones.

Later that year, Nicklaus went on to emphasize that he was back with a truly dominant performance in the US PGA. One off the lead after two rounds, he took the championship by the scruff of the neck with a 66, which was achieved despite dropping two shots over the last four holes. Three strokes in the lead, he then finished in 69 to win by seven from Andy Bean. Only four players broke 70 on the final day, and none except Nicklaus were contenders.

Five years on, Nicklaus remains a major golfer. He no longer enters any event as the automatic favourite – that position now goes to Watson, or Ballesteros and perhaps Bernhard Langer. He remains a likely winner, however, as he showed with his victory in the Memorial Tournament at Muirfield Village, his own course, at Dublin, Ohio, in 1984. If Jack chooses to continue playing, I'd wager it will be some years yet before his competitive appearances become purely ceremonial.

From his record, there's no doubt that of those who've been at the top for, say, 15 or 20 years, Jack Nicklaus is the greatest golfer of all time. What qualities, however, have made him so great? As I've pointed out, there have always been flaws in his game, principally in short pitching and bunker play. In none of the other stroke-playing departments does he stand alone either, though it would be hard to pick his superior as a striker

This putt didn't go in. The 1980 US Open which Jack won

of the long-irons or the man more likely to hole a putt when it really matters.

Nicklaus himself thinks his most important motivation is the desire to avoid embarrassment. This may sound odd, so let me explain what he means. Jack, quite simply, takes great pride in his performance. He wants every finish in a tournament and every shot to be good ones. Even if Nicklaus is way out of contention, his last round is still likely to be round about par, just simply because he doesn't want to be seen limping home in 75. If he were to have a 75, 75, 75 start, it would make him all the more determined to finish with a 65.

But the avoidance of embarrassment, whatever Jack may say, can only be part of the story. For instance, he had no other youthful ambitions except to be a very good golfer indeed and while still in his teens, those ambitions shifted gear: he wanted to be the greatest golfer of all time, probably as early as his first victory in the US Amateur Championship in 1959. But many have been just as ambitious, had just as much desire to win. Nicklaus has kept his ambitions. With 19 major championships and 70 victories on the US Tour, he still wants to win. Others have seen the money pour in and have been satisfied. Who can blame them?

I believe that three factors have, however, been even more vital to his success. One, as Jack would call it, is course management; another, sheer nerve; the other a marvellous wife and strong family life.

Nicklaus gives detailed thought to how every hole should be played, almost like a military commander calculating the placement of the forces at his command and whether a full frontal assault is called for or a flank attack. Strategy decided, he sticks to it and is just as dangerous a competitor when not swinging and striking well. As he says: 'Day in and day out I'm a better strategist and tactician than I am a shot maker. I've had the ability to win when playing poorly.' The reverse of this coin is that Nicklaus believes that even when striking the shots at his best he is apt to lose if he allows himself to become exhilarated and stops thinking. But does it, I wonder, in the end come down to nerve? Is Nicklaus the most gifted of them all at carrying on playing the shots in the heat of the final hour of a major championship? As he has said himself: 'While some championships are won, most of them are lost. What I've really done is failed a little less than other people who have had a chance to win.'

NICKLAUS, JACK WILLIAM
Born: Columbus, Ohio, USA, 21 January 1940
Major championship victories: 1959 US Amateur Championship;
1961 US Amateur Championship; 1962 US Open Championship;
1963 US Masters, US PGA Championship; 1965 US Masters; 1966
US Masters, British Open Championship; 1967 US Open
Championship; 1970 British Open Championship; 1971 US PGA
Championship; 1972 US Open Championship, US PGA
Championship; 1973 US PGA Championship; 1975 US Masters, US
PGA Championship; 1978 British Open Championship; 1980 US
Open Championship, US PGA Championship.
Ryder Cup player: 1969, 1971, 1973, 1975, 1977, 1981
US Tour victories (1962–84): 70
Overseas victories (1962–78): 18

Total career victories (1962–84): 88
US Tour money winnings (1962–84): $4,520,824
European Tour money winnings (1962–84): £103,063
World career money winnings (1962–84): $5,521,620

LEE

TREVINO

For the large majority of our Supreme Champions, the road to the top was long, with much stalling along the way. The early career of Lee Buck Trevino, however, is unique. He didn't attempt the US Tour until his late twenties because he didn't think he was good enough and in this way is similar only to Britain's Brian Waites.

Trevino came from much the most 'disadvantaged' background of any of our Supremes. Born in 1939, he never knew his father, also called 'Lee' and was brought up by his mother, Juanita Trevino, and his grandfather. Neither could read nor write. For a time they lived in a four-roomed shack, near Dallas, Texas, which had no electricity, plumbing or even windows. He began playing golf at the age of eight, first knocking horse apples about with a broomstick and then helping out at a driving range where he became the protégé of the owner, Hardy Greenwood, who was later to give Trevino his first full set of golf clubs. He was also the greatest influence on Trevino's development as a golfer and a father figure. Trevino was entirely self-taught, which was perhaps the main reason why he developed such an eccentric golf swing. There was no one to tell Lee this or that was wrong, so he continued on his way. It didn't look pretty but it worked.

At 14, he had to leave school, where he was reckoned to be outstandingly athletic and went to work full time at the driving range. Soon he left to work for a country club but moved on at the age of 17 to serve in the Marines for four years. A good deal of his time was spent playing golf with the officers. In 1960, he became a golf professional, working as an assistant in El Paso, Texas. His competitive schooling mostly involved money matches for fairly small amounts which he couldn't afford to lose. Sometimes there were bets where Trevino had to miss every green and rely on chipping and putting for his pars. Once, he spent a year practising with a Dr Pepper bottle and claims he didn't lose a single match in the following three years on a par-3 course.

He knew nothing of the outside world of big money golf. He played in local competitions, mostly pro ams, and learned the sales patter of the pro's shop and this was to prove very useful when the good years came. Immediately, he was able to establish a rapport with Press and golf galleries alike and was much in demand for exhibitions and company days. It's all very well being a good golfer but it helps if you can have an easy patter and ready smile.

In 1965 there came a turning point for Trevino. He won a rather more important local competition, the Texas State Open, and was also second in the Mexican Open. The following year he qualified for the US Open. Although, in finishing fifty-fourth, he was totally unnoticed he had at least made the break. It was further proof that he could compete at a high level. That same year, he played a couple of rounds in money matches with Raymond Floyd and won them both.

Trevino's confidence rose higher the following year. His second wife, Claudia, entered him for the 1967 US Open at Baltusrol. Trevino scored very steadily indeed, having rounds of 72, 70, 71 and 70. With a round to go, he was three strokes behind the leaders. His closing round of 70 was anything but a disgrace but neither he nor anyone else came close to matching Jack Nicklaus's 65 finish.

Still, Trevino had finished alone in fifth place and had $6,000 to take home. He was encouraged to play more tournaments that year and had his best placing of fourth in the Canadian Open. At the advanced age of 28 he was Rookie of the Year, a title given to the first-year player who wins the most money on the US Tour. In Trevino's case this was a little over $26,000. For the first time, he became a full PGA member. He knew he could compete with the best and decided to play the Tour full time in 1968. To the public, and most of his fellow professionals, he remained an unknown.

All that changed at the Oak Hill Country Club in New York State, site of the 1968 US Open. The rough was very severe 'like a racoon's nest', as Sam Snead said and these were conditions which suited Trevino down to the ground. He is a relatively short hitter and at the time reckoned to be able to hit much the same distance with a driver as Jack Nicklaus could achieve with a 3-iron. He was not a straight hitter in the real sense but rejoiced in a well-nigh infallible banana slice. It meant Trevino could aim down the left rough and bring the ball back to the fairway. All the trouble on the left was blocked out by a rather ugly but highly repetitive swing.

At Oak Hill, he began with rounds of 69 and 68, to lead the favourite, Jack Nicklaus by five strokes. He was hardly missing a fairway (just one, he claimed after his first round), playing for safety in his shots into the greens and holing his fair share of putts.

However, another man had an apparently firmer grasp on the championship, Bert Yancey, who was a leading American golfer of the time, with a special passion to win a major championship and a great student of the golf swing and the history of golf. After the second day, with rounds of 67 and 68, he led Trevino by two strokes, and had set what was then a record for the halfway stage of the US Open. These two played together for the remainder of the championship. Early in the third round, things began to swing Yancey's way. With ten holes played, he had increased his lead over Trevino to five strokes. At this point, Trevino made a strong move, with birdies at three of the next four holes. Yancey dropped a shot late on in the round and at the end of the day his lead had almost gone: 205 to Trevino's 206.

In the Press Tent afterwards, Trevino obviously enjoyed his new found fame – as he has done ever since. He was full of confidence in three vital aspects of the game: driving, putting and 'scrambling'. If he missed a green badly, he felt he could still manage to finish in two more strokes. If his confidence wasn't misplaced, he just about had the championship in his grasp: the man who can drive and putt is a match for anyone. The scrambling was a welcome bonus.

For the final day, there were just the three men in it: Trevino himself, Yancey, the leader, and Nicklaus, who was set to throw caution to the winds and go for the flag instead of safe areas on the greens. Nicklaus, playing ahead, made an early move, with birdies that cut into the lead. His driving was thunderous, his approach shots precise – but he just couldn't hole the putts. Soon it was apparent that the contest was really between Yancey and Trevino.

Both began poorly, but Trevino seemed to settle to the task after a scrambling par at the 2nd. With Nicklaus too far behind and Yancey's play now lacking its earlier assurance, Trevino, aided by birdie putts just after the turn, had the championship in his pocket if he could just hold on.

The last two holes demonstrated that Lee's confidence in his scrambling abilities were well justified. He completely mishit a long-iron to the 17th but compensated by stroking a long putt home. At the last, the championship won, he drove into the rough, tried to reach the green with a mid-iron and left his ball in the rough. From a poor lie, he hit flat out with a wedge, hoping to move the ball somewhere near the green. It settled 3 feet from the hole. That was that. Trevino had a 69, his fourth round below par and he became, and remains, the only competitor in the US Open to have four rounds under 70.

It was clear that a new personality had arrived. Here was a golfer who could talk, give a stream of quotable material in the Press Tent and was able to quip with his galleries. Whether Trevino was a new star in the firmament was far more a matter of doubt. He had his major championship. Could he do it again? If Trevino himself thought he had a 'bad swing', no one doubted him. The British golf writer Leonard Crawley described it as 'agricultural' and I myself thought that he might prove a one-tournament flash in the pan, like at least two other post-war US Open winners, Jack Fleck in 1955 and Orville Moody, a friend of Trevino's, who was to win in 1969. On the other hand, Peter Thomson was more impressed with the way Trevino had handled the pressure. He thought Trevino's victory was a very convincing performance and said: 'I have no doubt he could do it again.'

The Trevinos were soon on the move from a tiny apartment to a grand Spanish-style house. The money began to flow in but the doubts remained about his peculiar swing. It had worked once in the cockpit of a major championship, would it do so again? Let us now pause to examine Lee's swing in some detail. The starting point is that he's a natural hooker of the ball who has learned, in the years after leaving the Marines, to move the ball from left to right. He was inspired to do so by watching Ben Hogan play, realizing how much safer this shape of shot is as I also came to realize myself quite early on in my own tournament career.

Rather oddly, Trevino attempted all this without changing his grip one jot. Although a good one, his left-hand position on the club is rather strong and the right-hand V pointing to the right shoulder, is very different from many current good players who have both Vs pointing somewhere between the chin and halfway to the right shoulder.

At the top of the backswing, Trevino doesn't have the toe of the club aiming along the target line. Instead, the head is just about square on, a recipe for pulling and hooking the ball to the left. How then does Trevino avoid this?

At the address, he stands very open to the target line at about 45 degrees, which is more extreme than any competent player I've ever seen. Now, I'm not talking about tournament players but rather the level of club golfers who are highly delighted to break 80 with the aid of some inspired putting. If you saw him setting up on your club's practice ground you might indeed think he was a new member and stroll over to give him a

This man changes his putters. This was a favourite in 1980

few tips about how to line up. He also has his ball opposite the left toe for long shots.

As Trevino starts the clubhead away from the ball, naturally enough he begins along the line of his feet, away and out from the intended line of flight. Soon, however, he pushes the club even further away outside the target line, but moves his right hip slightly to the right which brings his arms almost on line. Yet, it's still almost a recipe for total disaster, a flat quick hook and if the man weren't a genius . . . Next, he begins to move the club very much around his body and reaches the top with the clubface shut, as I've said earlier. Despite the open stance, Trevino is still all set to duckhook the ball. Sometimes he does, but very rarely. The reason he doesn't, soon follows. Trevino then does everything humanly possible to slice the ball. Most of it comes from the legs driving along the line of swing, hands ahead of the clubhead. The rest is a result of quelling wrist action so that Trevino only allows it to intrude if he wants to hook the ball.

Trevino in play during the 1981 Ryder Cup at Walton Heath against Sam Torrance (watching). who lost by five and three

Otherwise, the swing movement is dominated by the thought that the clubface must be either open or square at impact. He manages this by the most pronounced leg action and pulling movement of the clubhead ever seen in golf. The clubhead is far too squared off at the top of the swing; it must, at best, not deteriorate in the hitting area to avoid a very sharp hook. Trevino does the trick by leading with his legs, keeping the hands dead still and pulling the clubhead into the ball with his left side. The whole sequence is almost totally a pulling action of the left side.

Trevino says himself that he only manages it by too much body movement, a very pronounced slide of the hips along the target line with an accompanying sway in the same direction. Trevino thinks his method has something to offer handicap golfers. I just don't believe it, unless they too are geniuses.

It all produces a great deal of stress on the lower back region, where he's experienced many aches and pains for at least the last ten years. Trevino's highly unconventional body movements also seemed to need a great deal of repetitive work on the practice ground to keep the machine in fighting trim. Trevino certainly thought so and, after he'd reached the top, spent far more hours hitting balls than most great players have done, just to keep his confidence going. Later, we'll see what happened when strict medical necessity reduced him to hitting just a few balls before going out on the course.

What I've described so far, would convince no one at all that Trevino has an effective golf swing. But in the hitting area he has a great plus. The clubhead travels low along the target line for that vital fraction of a second longer. With Hogan, it was achieved by a thrust of the right hand and forearm through the ball; with Trevino, right side quiet, left side pulling, the result is much the same flat-bottomed arc in the hitting area.

Yet the mechanics are just a part of golf and many years ago I came to believe that they had far less to do with success at golf than I might have wished. It's not the best swings that produce success but the ones that can be maintained, imperfect though they may seem to the onlooker, and here Trevino scores very highly indeed. Some of his movements are so extreme that it must make it easier for him to feel them. Certainly he claims that he is always aware of the position of his clubhead throughout the swing.

However, despite his US Open victory, some time passed before Trevino was fully established as one of the great players of modern times. Perhaps this happened in 1970 when he was top money earner. The following year he became an international star. He started with a couple of US Tour wins but when he arrived at Merion for the US Open he was still not entirely sure how good he was and had not won a major championship since Oak Hill three years before.

His performance was very convincing. After tying with Jack Nicklaus, he went on to beat him by 68 to 71 in the play-off. Trevino's relatively short but accurate driving had proved highly suited to Merion, a very tight course with punishing rough. It's one of my greatest favourites, though no monster at 6,500 yards and par-70. He was helped by some uncharacteristic errors from Nicklaus, who left two bunker shots in sand during his 71 and also, according to Trevino, 'chilli dipped' two wedge shots (for non-Americans, I ought to explain this means a duff, stab or fluff).

At the end of it all, Nicklaus commented to Trevino: 'You just don't know how good you are. You can win anywhere.' So Trevino went off to Canada and won the Canadian Open and then moved on to Royal Birkdale to compete in his third British Open Championship. After three rounds the year before, at St Andrews, he had looked the likely winner but had a last round of 77 to tie for third place behind Nicklaus and Doug Sanders.

Trevino gives thanks for a
putt that dropped

Trevino began with some typical scrambling. Playing his first nine holes, he missed four fairways and both the par-3 greens but was still out in 33, having used his putter just 11 times. He came in with a 69 and was at the top of the leader board with three other players of whom Tony Jacklin, then at the height of his powers, posed the greatest threat.

The next day, both had 70s and led the field. Trevino's putter was again a magic wand, with four putts of indecent length holed. For the third round, they were paired together and Trevino was displeased when British cheers rang out for their fellow countryman, his own best efforts being greeted with polite clapping. Nevertheless, his round of 69 put him one ahead of Jacklin and Liang Huan Lu, with whom he played the last round.

If Trevino's putting had saved him many shots up to that point, he was inspired on the outward nine, which he covered in 31 strokes, single-putting seven of the first eight greens. He had the championship sewn up, or so it seemed, with a four-stroke lead. He remarked later: 'It was so much fun I almost forgot to finish the tournament.'

That lack of concentration caught up with him on the 17th. Instead of the customary fade, Trevino hit high into the sand dunes on the left and found a buried lie. He took a violent slash at the ball but moved it only a yard or so, and still in loose sand. From a better lie, he then flew his ball across the fairway into the rough. He took seven on the hole. Not many have won with such a score on the card in their last round – Jones at Hoylake in 1930, Thomson in 1955 and Bill Rogers in 1981 the notable exceptions. Trevino was also successful. With his lead reduced to just one stroke at the 18th, he coasted a long putt just inches past the hole and par was good enough. He had won three national open championships in little more than a month.

By now, he had developed a taste for links golf. Playing with the small ball which he considered 'almost like cheating', his low flight has always made him a good wind player. Not a long hitter, he usually finds British links courses hard and running so he can get up at the par-5s with his second shots running to greens he couldn't carry. He has said to me so often that he loves to 'bump and run 'em'.

All very different from Augusta National and the Masters, where Trevino has never done well, often turning down invitations to play in earlier days. Many of the holes dogleg right to left, favouring tee-shots with draw. Trevino says hooked iron shots are also needed to hold shots into the left to right slopes of most of the greens. One year, he made a determined effort and practised for a couple of weeks to change the shape of his iron shots to a draw; he led the championship after two rounds, but then dropped back. Of course, he can draw his shots at will, just as Bobby Locke could fade the ball but it never felt natural, was less accurate and very difficult to sustain for shot after shot.

Trevino also thinks that his fairly short hitting is too heavily penalized at Augusta. His tee-shots pitch and stop in the upslopes others carry.

Finally, there is the problem that, unlike on British links, he cannot run the ball to the greens on long holes with his second shot. There is far less run on the ball and, often, a water hazard or huge bunker blocking the way.

Many golfers who used to play Augusta were unable to reach the par-5s in two, or indeed decided to play conservatively, hoping to get their birdies from a good pitch and a putt. This is no longer the case. Yearly the pace quickens. It's a limitation of Trevino's game that he has to give away so much length to the rest of the field at Augusta and other courses where long carrying shots to the green are essential.

Trevino returned to Britain for the 1972 Open Championship at Muirfield brimming with confidence, an event which was to 'finish' Tony Jacklin but did Trevino no harm at all. Ballesteros was thought lucky after his first championship at Royal Lytham in 1979, and Trevino's win in 1972 is also remembered in Britain as more than 'lucky', even the most outrageous victory of all time. With good reason perhaps, but they all count. That year, Nicklaus was on the crest of a wave. He held the US PGA Championship from the previous year and in 1972 had won both the Masters and the US Open. Could he do the Grand Slam, all four majors in one calendar year, a feat never done and only approached by Ben Hogan in 1953?

At the end of the second day, Jacklin and Trevino were tied for the lead with such names as Nicklaus, Player, Miller and Sanders only a stroke behind. Trevino began his third round with no fireworks, reaching the turn in level par and keeping it up over the next four holes. Then things began to happen. He holed a fair length putt on the 14th and a much longer one on the 15th. At the 16th, a par-3, he was bunkered short of the green, towards the rear and on a downslope. It was a difficult shot and Trevino came down too sharply on it. His ball came out far too strong – perhaps thinned – and headed for the bunkers on the opposite side of the green. But at least it had one virtue, the shot was straight and, almost unbelievably, it clattered into the flagstick and fell into the hole. A birdie, which could well have been a 4 or even a 5. The 17th, a par-5, was easily reachable that day and he birdied that hole also. At the last, a very tough finishing hole, Trevino went through to the fringe, some 15 yards or more from the hole. From there, he chipped his ball in for his fifth consecutive birdie and a round of 66.

Nicklaus now seemed out of touch, six strokes behind, but Jacklin, who partnered Trevino that day, had withstood the onslaught bravely. His 67 left him just a stroke behind. Surely the final day would be a contest between England's golfing hero and Lee Trevino. The odds looked on Jacklin. He'd missed his share of short putts but, in that third round, had consistently put his iron shots inside Trevino's.

The final day at Muirfield in 1972 was one of the most memorable in all the long history of the British Open Championship. Nicklaus, far behind, reached the turn in 32 and then birdied the next 2 holes: 11 holes, and just 38 strokes. At this point he led the championship. For the rest, he played well but had no more birdies and dropped a shot on the 16th. He was round in 66 and had set the target.

Meanwhile, Jacklin and Trevino matched each other shot for shot and they came to the 17th tee with the American's one-stroke lead still intact. Jacklin began with a good drive and a second shot some 20 yards short of the green and perhaps 50 yards from the hole at this par-5. Meanwhile, Trevino's tee-shot was pulled into a bunker and, after playing out, he was still well short in three and in thickish rough. He hacked rather hurriedly at it and his ball ran through the green and up a bank. At last it was Jacklin's turn, with Trevino through in four and Tony just short in two. He pitched reasonably well but had a putt of 15 feet or so for a birdie. Trevino, after seeing his fourth shot, had written off his title chances. 'I've thrown it away,' he remarked. He looked along the line of his chip quickly and played almost impatiently as after all, the day was lost, but suddenly it became very interesting once more. His ball was running at the hole, well paced and down it went. A par-5 after all with three of the shots poor ones.

With the benefit of hindsight, you could say that that Trevino chip was the end of Jacklin's career at the very top of world golf. He three-putted and then dropped another stroke on the last to finish third behind Jack Nicklaus. It was Trevino's fourth major championship.

Another came his way at Tanglewood in North Carolina in 1974, the US PGA. Again Jack Nicklaus featured, the holder of the championship. In wet conditions, it was interesting to see that Trevino was getting the same length with his tee-shots. Nicklaus's drives soared upwards, plummeted down and stopped. Trevino's low-flighted shots skipped along the wet fairways for many more yards after pitching. They both finished with 69s, which left Trevino with a one-stroke victory, despite, he says, nerves which made his putter jump in his hands on the last green.

In the years 1970 to 1974, Trevino was never out of the top four on the US money list. For several years after there was a slight decline, perhaps caused by lower back problems which seem to date from his being struck by lightning during the 1975 Western Open. He had an operation in 1976, but it seemed to do little good. Financial disaster came two years later when unwise management and investments left him having to try to make another fortune and this he set about doing, helped by the fact that his tournament money winnings were supplemented by overseas appearance fees around $50,000, company days, exhibitions plus endorsement contracts for beer, tyres and golf equipment. Trevino has a colourful personality and a ready tongue while so many up-and-coming players on the US Tour didn't.

Trevino had his next big year in 1980, with three US tournaments under his belt and the lowest stroke average for 30 years. It brought him $385,000 on the US Tour and he also had a run at a major championship once again, the 1980 British Open at Muirfield, which he began with rounds of 68 and 67 to lead by three strokes before Tom Watson's third round of 64 more or less settled the championship. Trevino was second. By this time into his forties, and still troubled by his back, he fell away to 113th on the 1982 US money list and had an operation to deaden nerve ends in his back, which was a success, providing he gave up hitting hundreds of practice balls.

Semi-retired. Lee Trevino wins the 1984 US PGA Championship at Shoal Creek. Birmingham. Alabama in fine style

By 1984, his fortunes restored, Trevino seemed to have his sights set on public relations and TV work, though he declared he hadn't lost his golf game. He played only 16 tournaments in the States, one of them the PGA Championship at the Shoal Creek Golf Club in Alabama, a Nicklaus-designed course, which put a premium on driving accuracy, for the ball always seemed to settle well down in the semi-rough, making long recoveries well-nigh impossible.

Trevino had married for the third time in November 1983, by co-incidence, to a second Claudia who had revived a waning determination to succeed, telling him to 'Get off this "too old" business. Your golf clubs have no idea how old you are.' As so often, a new putter also comes into my story. Having putted poorly in the British Open, Trevino decided that a putter bought shortly after during the Dutch Open might be the answer. He slammed it on the floor of his hotel room as hard as he could and 'stomped it with my heel'. That took care of the fine tuning. He had adjusted the loft and lie. Ah yes, so many golf professionals are also master craftsmen! But it worked.

Trevino, as in his first major championship victory, produced four rounds in the 60s, and was in contention throughout. In the third round he reached the turn in 30 and at the end of the day led Lanny Wadkins by one stroke, and another old-time great, Gary Player, by two. That lead would have been more comfortable if he hadn't hooked an iron shot into water at the last hole.

In the final round, Trevino's putter immediately gave him a birdie from as much as 70 feet. At times, it looked as if Wadkins might overhaul Trevino – at the age of 44 would his nerve hold? However, on the 16th, he holed a vital par putt from some 4 yards and on the next Wadkins's hopes perished when he sent his tee-shot into the rough. Trevino played the final hole with a two-stroke lead – and increased it to four. It was a notable triumph and his first win of any kind since 1981. It all shows what a new putter, and a new wife, can do.

From his three marriages, Trevino has four children. How important are they to him? Well, as Trevino says: 'Golf has always been number one with me. Many times I've put it ahead of my family. I know that's not what people expect to hear. I could say I did it for the wife and kids. But that wouldn't be true.'

I believe Trevino's first motivation was to escape from poverty. This he'd already done by the time he began to play tournament golf and, so very quickly, found himself Open Champion of the USA, with that swing and method which had contrasted so strongly with the elegance of Bert Yancey as they played together through the final rounds.

Even so, of my Supreme Champions, his odd method succeeds as well as anyone's and it's worth speculating what he might have achieved if he'd gone into US Tour golf a few years earlier and had also begun with the desire to prove himself the greatest golfer of the time.

TREVINO, LEE BUCK
Born: Dallas, Texas, USA, 1 December 1939
Major championship victories: 1968 US Open Championship; 1971
US Open Championship, British Open Championship; 1972 British
Open Championship; 1974 US PGA Championship; 1984 US PGA
Championship.
Ryder Cup player: 1969, 1971, 1973, 1975, 1979, 1981
US Tour victories (1968–84): 27
Overseas victories (1971–83): 9
Total career victories (1968–84): 38
US Tour money winnings (1966–84): $3,037,092
European Tour money winnings (1969–84): £121,793
World career money winnings (1966–84): $4,192,617

TOM
WATSON

'We're vastly overrated.' That's part of Tom Watson's attitude to the fame and adulation that success brings to golfers (and all other athletes) today. It's always been very apparent to me that Tom is one of those who doesn't relish public attention and the praise of genuine admirers or hangers-on alike. True, he has the ambition to be recognized in golfing history as one of the greatest players but that's a very different matter from enjoying all the razzmatazz that goes hand-in-hand with being in the limelight. As I know only too well, much of that brings little more than occasional embarrassment, frequent boredom and always the feeling of being 'on parade' and having to put on a public face.

Indeed, when Tom is actually on parade as one of our Supreme Champions, in one respect he doesn't quite look the part. I'm sure he has a very lucrative clothing contract yet nothing seems to fit. The trousers are usually a touch too long or too short and the labelled shirts and polo necks too loose or too tight. All very different from, let's say, the casual elegance of Jack Nicklaus or Seve Ballesteros. Yet that same Jack Nicklaus 20 years and more ago, in jockey cap and khaki trousers could himself have been competing for the title of worst-dressed golfer. In Watson's case, such disregard for his attire has never been as openly contemptuous – after all, he belongs to a different era when nearly all conform to what is required of them and may well be fined by their PGAs if they don't!

The clothing contract is just one of several that brings Tom's income to something like $1½ million a year, a sum that dwarfs his tournament money winnings which give him a career total of about $4 million. In business, Watson has been very much his own man. It's a family affair with his wife Linda playing a major role though his manager is Charles Rubin, a lawyer who also happens to be Watson's brother-in-law.

Financially, Tom is obviously set up for life but his motivation remains as strong as ever. On the US Tour he restricts himself to about 20 events a year out of the more than 40 possible. He plays more than Jack Nicklaus and Johnny Miller – but not by that wide a margin. Watson's overseas appearances are limited. Of course, the British Open has absolute priority, Watson's favourite and best event, and he is also to be seen from time to time in Australia and Japan. But that's about it. He has learned to protect 'the property', devising a limited schedule which keeps him keen to play golf and competitively sharp.

Of the great and nearly great players, Watson realized early that the majors are what count and was later to say, 'Charisma is winning major championships'. A waning Johnny Miller may declare that a golfer's record in other tournaments is almost as important but, to be blunt, Miller will be remembered for winning the 1973 US Open and the 1976 British Open Championship far more than for the 22 US Tour events he has won to date or even for those couple of years when he played golf at a standard never seen before or since.

Tom appears to me to be a British Open specialist. Oddly he had won the championship a couple of times before he really understood what was involved or the armoury needed to combat the difficulties of seaside golf. At Carnoustie in 1975, he made his first appearance in Britain, with only two tournament wins under his belt. Surely he had no thoughts of winning as he went to the 1st tee? Yet there Watson produced a performance that has from time to time been a sort of trademark – keep going and it could be the others who will falter. Watson finished a little ahead of the apparent leading contenders and, lo and behold, they all came back to him – Bobby Cole, Johnny Miller, Jack Nicklaus, Neil Coles, and, of course, Jack Newton.

The play-off between this Australian and Watson swung to and fro. It could have gone either way but it was Watson who got his par on the last hole to win. He was on his way and has never looked back, at times making the British Open Championship and dominance of the US money list seem his by right.

I'm sure that victory took Tom Watson by surprise and he was a far more polished player at Turnberry in 1977, a championship which saw the most sustained man-to-man combat since the championship began in 1860. By this time, Watson was a very different player. If the 1975 championship had almost stolen up on him unawares, in 1977 he had come to believe in himself as the most effective scorer in the game of golf. He also sought perfection and, after the third round, was quick to point out to the Press that his 65 was better fashioned than Jack Nicklaus's had been with more tee-shots on the fairway and superior quality of strike on the irons. He didn't mention the putting and hardly needed to for, I believe, Watson is far and away the greatest short putter among the moderns, while his firm-wristed stroke from long range is also highly effective at keeping the ball on line to the holeside and is allied to unrivalled judgement of pace.

Watson is not the thinking man's perfect player. He certainly hits a long ball but some are rather wild. His very strong 'Popeye' forearms should give him an edge in long- and mid-iron play but, if you'll believe the statistics, he virtually never features in the US Tour figures for getting on the greens in regulation figures. In this department Nicklaus, among many others, earns much higher ratings.

That acute observer, Lee Trevino, claims that Tom hasn't got a soft shot. Everything is played with much the same firm, crisp rhythm. Lee believes that Tom can't pitch in with a high fading pattern of flight, that he has, basically, to bang everything at the flag. Well, they used to say that a certain Gardner Dickinson was more concerned about the shape of a particular shot and would be far more delighted to get a delicate fade or a low-drawn ball to 40 feet than something a little more direct nearer the pin. There are players more intent on the perfection of shot than the result, with Tom Weiskopf a clear example. I pass on the truth of these opinions

Ballesteros had made his 4 on the Road Hole at St Andrews in the 1984 British Open Championship. Few get down in two from here. Watson didn't and lost the title

but I can say that I've never seen anyone, lack of a soft shot or not, more adept at getting it close from around the green and then ramming home the putt, almost as an effort of will. His fellow players tend to think that if, at every hole, everyone missed all the greens, Watson would proceed to win all the tournaments. There may be better putters, chippers and pitchers. But no one else can put it all together as well.

Part of this has to do with practice. So many players go to the practice ground occupied with thoughts of the total golf swing. Will that tip about arching the left wrist just a little bit more work? Should the club be kept low to the ground on the backswing for an extra 6 inches? Well you know it all. Tournament golfers seek the magic solutions just as eagerly as the ordinary club player.

Watson goes through the same drills. But he is not so strong a believer. He'd like to be perfect, like Ben Hogan before him, but is much more a realist. Watson knows that, driving the ball well over 250 yards, many of his tee-shots will finish in the rough. The target areas are narrower at that distance. He'll practise and improvise from that kind of territory as much as others will devote time to watching the flight of, let's say, a 7-iron nudged into a perfect lie. How few golfers do this, yet so many shots are, for example, played when the ball is well down in the grass, from worn and bare turf around a green or when the backswing is impeded by a bush, tree or a wall. Watson spends time practising in all these and many other situations. When he gets into them, he's been there before and knows how to cope. Rather like Walter Hagen before him, Tom expects to hit a few poor shots in a round and then briskly confronts the problem and gets on with it.

This briskness is very obvious in other departments of his play. He may not be quite so fast as Lanny Wadkins but there's very little in it. Watson decides on the kind of shot he'll play as he approaches his ball and then simply looks target, ball, target – and swings. And I can detect hardly any difference if he's 20 strokes behind the leaders in a run-of-the-mill tournament or in hot contention for a major championship.

Two shots at such times in recent major championships will go into golfing history. For both, Watson was as brisk as ever. Needing to par the tough closing hole at Royal Birkdale to win the Open Championship in 1983 and after hitting a poor drive at the 17th, Watson quickly fired his drive straight down the fairway. He was equally brisk playing a 2-iron, held up against the wind, which finished in the heart of the green, making two putts for victory a formality.

An even more famous shot had occurred a little over a year earlier at Pebble Beach in the US Open Championship. Nicklaus had completed his final round; Watson needed a par, par finish to tie over two difficult holes, a long par-3, followed by a par-5 with an intimidating tee-shot and played right around the cliff tops. Watson then proceeded to stand the situation on its head. For a start, he looked as if he'd lost the championship when his long-iron bounced into quite thick rough just to the left of the green.

The shot that won the 1982 US Open from the fringe of the 71st green at Pebble Beach

There seemed little or no chance that he could get his tiny pitch shot to stop near the hole. Instead, in it went for a 2 and Tom needed only par on the last to win. The birdie which followed was not necessary but he had won his first US Open by two.

Two quite different stories have been told since about this legendary pitch-in. The first is that a TV company approached Watson with the request that he attempt to re-enact the shot. Watson refused. Why? Well perhaps he didn't want to tarnish his image by failing. The second is that Tom has since tried to do it again and again for his own personal satisfaction – and failed, seldom getting within several feet. You pays your money and takes your choice.

Perhaps that 1982 US Open assured Tom of golfing immortality but it certainly took many observers of golf a long time to concede him this status. Byron Nelson's opinion is interesting and he knows Tom's game better than anyone. He considers that Watson could prove to be better than both Hogan and Nicklaus, superior from the mid-irons through the pitching clubs and a far better clipper and putter. Although this argues supremacy for Watson in approach play and the short game only there's not much left for Hogan and Nicklaus to be good at is there? Just driving, fairway woods and the long-irons! They are departments of the game where Watson himself is no slouch.

Even so, shot-making was never Tom's main problem but learning to win and to manage both himself and the golf course was. He was introduced to golf at the age of six by his father but he did not have an outstanding amateur career. He won the Missouri State Amateur Championship four times and played for the Stanford University team for three years, finishing as their number one. He had no success at the higher levels of amateur golf, however, and with this record could hardly have been worth a thought as a possible Walker Cup choice.

The accepted route to the US Tour was a Walker Cup place and a proven record in national and regional amateur tournaments which players such as Nicklaus, Wadkins and Crenshaw have enjoyed as part of their golf pedigree. Nevertheless, Watson decided to try his luck on the US Tour and turned professional in 1971. His first season, 1972, was immediately reassuring.

The Bing Crosby National Pro-Am was the second event of the season, played over the testing courses of Pebble Beach, Spyglass Hill and Cyprus Point. Watson finished twentieth, seven strokes behind the play-off between Jack Nicklaus and Johnny Miller, winning a modest $1,400. It was a start and showed Tom that he could compete with the best. He won money in the next two or three events so in his first month on Tour he had gone a good way towards proving, if only to himself, that he could make a living at the game.

Learning to contend and to win were to take considerably longer. In the rest of the season by far his best result was second place in the Quad Cities

Open, his 69 and 66 finishing rounds putting him a stroke behind Deane Beman, now US Tour Commissioner. However, the field wasn't of the highest quality and Tom had yet to face the test of being tournament leader and holding onto it with all the big guns there.

That problem came twice in 1973. In the Hawaiian Open he took a three-stroke lead into the final round but then faltered to end with a 75. Much the same happened in the World Open, a strange and short-lived event dedicated to the idea that eight rounds of golf are a better test than four. In the fifth round, Watson played the splendid Pinehurst Number 2 course in 62, which catapulted him into a six-stroke lead, but he dribbled it away with rounds of 76, 76 and 77. However, by the end of the year he'd moved up from seventy-ninth place in the money list to thirty-fifth.

Watson first became a 'name' in 1974. The event which established him was the US Open at Winged Foot. After three rounds he was the leader by a stroke but on the final day staggered home with a 79. Three failures in a row. Among those in the know, it was openly bandied about that Tom Watson had no iron streak. He was a 'choker', a man who lost his nerve when protecting a lead. This reputation was only partly changed a short time later when Watson won for the first time at the Western Open. This time he had a weak third round but came past the leaders with a 69 on the last day to win by a couple of strokes from J. C. Snead and Tom Weiskopf.

He was by then an established player, and finished the year tenth in the US money list, which made him roughly equivalent to Ryder Cup status. In 1975 Tom Watson became a star but there were still problems along the way. After winning the Byron Nelson Classic in May, he had a second bad experience in the US Open at Medinah. His start of 67 and 68 equalled the championship record for the first 36 holes. Although his finish of 78 and 77 sounds like another total collapse it was a high-scoring event and his total of 290 was only three strokes worse than the winner's. (Lou Graham and John Mahaffey tied and Graham won the play-off.)

Later in the year, after his British Open title, Tom won the World Series and finished seventh on the US money list. Jack Nicklaus commented: 'He knows exactly where he's going. Straight ahead. Nothing distracts him. He has great abilities, super confidence and just enough cockiness. He's not a comer. He has arrived.'

Watson was indeed soon to take over from Jack Nicklaus as the world's leading player though that wasn't to be fully clear for some years yet. His progress was distinguished in the immediate future by being leading money winner four years in a row, 1977–80, with wins in the 1977 and 1981 Masters, but most of all by his extraordinary achievements in the British Open with five championship victories in the space of only nine years. If his victory at Turnberry over Jack Nicklaus remains the most memorable, Muirfield in 1980 saw Watson at another peak. After the first round he

Tom and Linda Watson
holding the trophy at
Muirfield in 1980

was tied for the lead with Lee Trevino and a 64 in the third round took him into a four-stroke lead. Thoughts of whether or not Watson might 'choke' were long gone. We all thought it was inevitable he would win. The final day was indeed rather dull as Tom put together a cast-iron 69 for a four-stroke victory.

By this time, Watson had made another move forward in the major championships. Almost always he was a contender, able to raise his game for the great occasions of golf even when not on his best form. Others may beat him, as Seve Ballesteros did when he started his final round so strongly in the 1983 Masters. Yet a month or so later, Watson produced form so devastating in the US Open as to leave the Spaniard in his wake. It should have been enough to give Watson his second US Open had that vast putt from 62 feet by Larry Nelson not gone in on the 16th hole.

If Tom has had to learn how to compete and withstand pressure, he has physically always been very well suited to the game. He has almost the perfect golfing body, with magnificent forearms and very strong legs, hands and shoulders and all at what I consider the right height, 5 feet 9 inches. If a player is 6 feet or more the game becomes more difficult. The angles are wrong and many players suffer from a lack of coordination. Short men, on the other hand, usually have insufficient power. Watson's physical fitness, like Nicklaus's, has also been vital. I can't remember him having any of the problems with his lower back, wrists and elbows that so many golfers suffer, Trevino and Fuzzy Zoeller, for instance, and whatever has become of those lady stars, Judy Rankin and Sally Little?

As he enters his mid-thirties, it's perhaps the right time to wonder where Watson will go from here. His desire, dedication and determination don't seem to have been diluted by all the success. Unlike so many, he still enjoys playing the game on both the sternly competitive and fun occasions. He was a great success in 1983 on BBC television's Pro-Celebrity series at Gleneagles and aroused great interest with his demonstration of the importance of the constant angle of the left elbow in putting. He could rattle several putts home from a few yards' range without needing to glance at the line again. Watson also enjoys playing with friends and declares he would still make trips to Britain and Ireland even if there were no British Open to play in. He declared Royal Dornoch the most fun he had ever had playing golf and said of the towering duneland of the great Ballybunion course in Western Ireland: 'Golf architects should live and play here before they build courses.'

Well past the horizontal on the backswing: the swing of a supple man

If Watson keeps that kind of enthusiasm, his tournament and championship successes ought to continue as long as that putting stroke remains firm and decisive. Here he's the early Arnold Palmer, willing to give the hole a chance from long range, confident that he'll be still able to hole those frightening 4- to 6-footers on the way back.

Watson is one of our Supreme Champions who seems to me to have very much benefited from the stability of his family life. It was typical that after his 1982 US Open Championship victory at Pebble Beach he didn't carouse away the night. Instead, he was to be seen on the rocks near the course quietly sharing a bottle of wine with his wife Linda and his two-year-old daughter, Meg. He has also remained in touch with his roots. Although he majored in psychology at Stanford University, he didn't seek the sun of either that state or, another favourite choice, Florida, once success came his way. The golfers who do so aren't necessarily sun-worshippers, of course. It's easier to keep a golf swing in trim during the off-season in warm weather, despite the fact that the golf season is now so long that it's certainly possible to play around the world in a summer climate throughout.

However, Watson has remained faithful to the American Mid-West and his birthplace Kansas City. In fact, he claims actually to enjoy bad weather golf and that has included playing in snow. It's all part of a pattern which has allowed Tom Watson to relish his success but to keep as level-headed as when he's contending for a major championship.

WATSON, THOMAS STURGES
Born: Kansas City, Missouri, USA, 4 September 1949
Major championship victories: 1975 British Open Championship;
1977 US Masters, British Open Championship; 1980 British Open
Championship; 1981 US Masters; 1982 US Open Championship,
British Open Championship; 1983 British Open Championship.
Ryder Cup player: 1977, 1981, 1983
US Tour victories (1974–84): 31
Overseas victories (1975–84): 7
US Tour money winnings (1971–84): $3,580,163
European Tour money winnings (1975–84): £169,183
World career money winnings (1971–84): $4,330,581

SEVERIANO
BALLESTEROS

I've sometimes been accused of hankering after the past. Some say I'm too attached to the great names of my youth, to the Hogans, Nelsons and Cottons, and to those a rung or two lower on the ladder of greatness in the game of golf. The latter include Jimmy Demaret, the Whitcombe brothers, Max Faulkner, Dai Rees as well as many other very good players who were either my contemporaries or mature players when I started out as a tournament player.

Well, it may be true. Like many of us I was an impressionable young man and I studied at the feet of these and so many other players who are no longer household names in the 1980s. Perhaps I was once a little slow to recognize the abilities of a Jack Nicklaus, a Gary Player, a Tom Watson or a Bernhard Langer.

However, I was never in any doubt at all about this young man from the Santander region in northern Spain and easily the most exciting player to watch since the very best days of Arnold Palmer. I could argue, and convincingly, that the Spaniard is the greatest player ever. I would do so even though Seve will never achieve the dominance of Byron Nelson on the US Tour at the end of the Second World War, the major championships of Jack Nicklaus and Bobby Jones or inspire the same awe that Ben Hogan did among both the players of his day and his galleries.

Yet, far more even than they, Seve Ballesteros has all the talents for playing the game of golf. Jack Nicklaus has declared him the longest hitter of the 1- and 2-iron ever. With the driver, he has curbed his youthful exhuberance, shortening his backswing a little, but remains capable of driving enormous distances when he needs the length. But sheer hitting power in golf has always been just a small part of the whole story. To experience all the rhythm and poetry of the golf swing, you could do no better than watch Seve strike the mid- and short-irons, when power is of no importance at all and balance and precision are everything.

However, this is a part of golf where it's just about impossible to assess the greatness of players. Even those ardent statisticians of the US Tour make no attempt to decide who is the most accurate in the shots at the flag. They content themselves with a 'Greens in Regulation' category, which, you could say, records who got there in the right number of strokes but provides no real evidence of how they did it or where they were. Often, part of the magic is keeping the ball out of the long stuff. Here, Seve has not been at all outstanding; few long hitters ever are.

The more controlled Ballesteros of the 1980s is still often off the fairway but has the bewilderingly fast hand action to not only escape from rather frightening lies but also to get the ball on the green. Interestingly, his game plan in winning two of his major championships included deliberately aiming for the rough off the tee, or so he claims. At Royal Lytham in 1979, he felt that the rough was not as severe as the pundits were saying and that he ought to think far more of keeping clear of fairway bunker trouble and of favourable lines in to the flag position on the day. A few years later, at St Andrews in 1984, he had a fairly similar thought: 'Keep out of the bunkers'. This led him to play his tee-shot towards 'safe' areas of the course, occasionally well clear of the hole in play. Indeed, why not? Golf can be a matter of deciding which is your own best route for getting from the 5th tee to the 5th green regardless of what the course architect or club committee long ago decided golfers ought to do.

So far, however, I haven't made out a watertight case that Seve is the greatest player alive today. That's because I haven't written as yet of the short game or the art of getting down in two from 20 to 50 yards.

Seve excels in visualizing the flight and run of the ball from near the green and deciding what kind of shot will result in his getting close. Should it be a high gentle lob, the clubhead slicing under the ball? Or, perhaps, better still to catch a slight upslope with a 7-iron chip and bump it to the holeside. He knows he can play all manner of variations. He is seldom far wrong in estimating his touch on the day or how the ball will behave when it meets both clubhead and turf.

As a putter he isn't among the all-time greats, high though his reputation is. For holing out from short range, you can sometimes see that he doesn't

This putt just missed at Oakmont during the 1983 US Open

quite totally trust that he can stuff the ball into the hole, in the 3- to 6-foot range. In the short game, he relies on feel and is really happier attempting to hole out from 4 to 6 yards or in coping with the problems of touch and judging the infuriating contours on such greens as St Andrews and Augusta National, where he sees so clearly how the ball will run at the hole.

I said earlier that Ballesteros has no superior in the rough but one other frequent cause of trouble is, of course, sand. Here Seve's rhythm, balance and feel for how the ball will run is among the best. Exact striking means that he can whisk the ball away in fairway bunkers from lies terrifying to others and near the green he has exceptional feel for how the clubhead will behave as it slices through the sand. Much of the feel is a legacy from his early days when he first tried swinging a golf club at the age of seven. It was a made-up club with a 3-iron head. The shafts, usually short-lived, were sticks. He soaked them in a bucket of water for an hour or two to make them swell to fit the hosel snugly. The seven-year-old then learned the feel of the clubhead through the swing and at impact – on stones, fir cones or whatever he chanced on. By the age of eight, he had a proper 3-iron and balls to hit, if he could find them at the Real Club de Golf de Pedrena, across the bay from Santander.

Golf was in Seve's blood. His father was Baldomero Ballesteros Presmanes and his mother's maiden name was Carmen Sota Ocejo. Sota is the most important of these names. His mother was the sister of one Ramon Sota, a man who had been the best golfer in all Spain for about ten years in the 1960s. He, too, was born at Pedrena; he, too, had been a caddie at the local golf club just after the Second World War. Ramon was a very different kind of player from Seve. He went into tournament golf with a very good short game but a weak long game, something he remedied over the years. A very slow player, he became the first tournament golfer to be penalized in Britain by the PGA for slow play, a fate never likely to befall Seve.

Although Ramon has started a tradition, Seve's three brothers were a much greater influence. Manuel, the eldest, was by far the most important in Seve's development and was a tournament player from 1967, when Seve had been trying his hand at golf for only a couple of years or so. Manuel became the youngster's model. Seve watched the way he swung a club and tried to imitate him though today the two are very different in style.

Even so, it's entirely possible to pick up many details of another player's swing and come up with a result that looks entirely different. A young player will latch onto, perhaps, a slow take-away, rhythm and balance, obviously active hands in the hitting area, a full shoulder turn – any of these things plus many more – and fit and adapt what he sees into a swing that remains his own.

Seve's progress was rapid – as it has been for so many youngsters whose hopes have come to nothing. At the age of 12 he broke 80 for the first time, so often a barrier for the aspiring young. Seve was on his way and down to scratch the same season. The next year, he beat Manuel for the first time, yet another milestone, and by the age of 14 was doing it often.

Family influence now became decisive in giving Seve confidence. His mother began to declare that he'd be the best player in the world and his brothers Baldomero, Vicente and Manuel recognized it also, without a hint of envy. Since then, Manuel has been his only real coach and still helps Seve analyse defective movements in his swing.

At 16 years and 8 months, Seve turned pro, making him the youngest ever to do so in Spain. He began to play tournaments in 1974, his first competition being the Spanish PGA. He failed to qualify three times but then won his first event, the Spanish Under-25 Championship. In the year, he won a useful £3,000. Further progress followed in 1975 when he rose to twenty-sixth in the Order of Merit, but remained unnoticed, except by Roberto de Vicenzo who talked widely of his tremendous promise. He had begun the 1976 season with top six finishes in both the Portuguese and Spanish Opens but in an early appearance on mainland Britain began with rounds of 84 and 78 in the PGA Championship at Royal St George's and, not surprisingly, he failed to qualify. He was equally unnoticed when the Open Championship came to Carnoustie that year, again not making the last 36 holes. But the Open Championship was soon to prove the event that brought him to world notice and sent him on his way, once and for all.

At Royal Birkdale, Seve began with a round of 69, which tied him for the lead with two others. But none of them, Christy O'Connor Junior, Norio Suzuki of Japan or Seve was expected to be heard of from after the second round. And when Ballesteros set out on his second round, such thoughts seemed fully justified. On the first nine he dropped several strokes. He began to pick up birdies on the homeward journey. After a fine finish, he had another 69 and stood two strokes ahead of Johnny Miller who was in second place.

The young Spaniard was paired with Miller for the rest of the championship. In the third round, he again made a poor start. It allowed Miller to draw alongside and then go 2 clear at the turn. Ballesteros countered first with a birdie and then a vast hook at the 11th. When he found his ball, he had to ask the direction of the green but got it there with his second shot and drew level again with the American. By the end of the round, helped by an eagle at the 17th, he had restored a two-stroke lead over Miller. A legend was in the making. Already, they were beginning to write and talk of Ballesteros as a huge hitter who was both powerful and adept in recovery play. And boy could he putt.

It began to seem, after Seve's recovery over the second nine, when so many might have collapsed, that a man just three months past his nineteenth birthday could become Open Champion. It was, however, not to be. Miller, with a last round 66, won the championship and with Spanish errors to help him certainly had an unassailable lead after he'd eagled the

13th hole. Ballesteros, however, finished well, all pars and a birdie on the 14th and then an eagle on the 17th. A shot he played on the 18th remains the most remembered one of that championship. It was not in any way the most spectacular shot Ballesteros had played but it came when Seve needed to be down in two to tie Jack Nicklaus for second place. Short and left in two, he was faced with little green to play with, so that a lofted pitch shot would not get him close. Instead, he played a running 9-iron into the upslope short of the green and between two bunkers to about 4 feet. Graciously, Miller putted out, leaving Ballesteros to play the final shot of the 1976 Open Championship on centre stage, a position he's occupied more often than not ever since.

However well you can play your shots, either at club or tournament level, confidence is much more important. If the world thought Seve Ballesteros might have arrived, the Spaniard *knew* he had. Within a month, he had won his first tournament, the Dutch Open, and a little later he took the Lancôme in France. The manner of that victory is part of the Ballesteros legend. With nine holes left to play, Arnold Palmer held a four-stroke lead. He did little wrong over the homeward stretch, hitting every green in regulation. But Seve did better, having five birdies for a 31 home and a one-stroke victory.

Towards the end of the year, he partnered Manuel Pinero in a Spanish World Cup victory and was in tears when Manuel holed the putt which ensured their success. Seve's patriotism has, some say, been found wanting since. Why, Spaniards interested in golf ask, does our best player usually refuse to play for his country? Well, there was once a time, in the Canada Cup days of old, when Bernard Hunt and I would turn out for England, Nicklaus and Palmer for the USA and Thomson and Nagle for Australia. But in more recent years, many of the greats don't come. They prefer to stay at home, or go elsewhere. The prize money is poor, appearance money token and if Spain, the USA or, let's say, Nicaragua win, there isn't the feeling that the winners represent the greatest golfing nation on Earth.

The attitude of the Spanish public towards his golfing achievements has given vent to the occasional grouse from Seve. Although there are only around 40,000 golfers in Spain, he does feel that the Spanish should care more and that the media takes little interest in golf as a minority sport. As Seve punched the sky again and again exultantly, as his birdie putt on the 72nd hole at St Andrews made the 1984 Open Championship his for certain, was Spanish television there? No. A little time was given on television in Spain to a victory that had fixed him for ever among the all-time greats of golf on a later sports' highlights show. In Spain, he is just a little more celebrated than, say, a British World champion marbles player.

Seve, then, is not motivated by any notion that he is 'doing it for Spain'. With world-wide money winnings of now well over $2 million and money pouring in, perhaps $1 million a year, exhibitions, endorsements, company

Ballesteros exults as his birdie putt drops at the last hole in the 1984 Open Championship at St Andrews. No one in the field remained in reach and it was one of the most joyous moments in golf I've ever seen

days, advertising fees and much else, that too should no longer be a spur to further achievement. His financial future has been very secure since his twenty-fourth year, when he'd added the 1980 US Masters to his 1979 British Open. If one major championship doesn't make you a millionaire, two make it just about unavoidable!

So, for Seve, I believe the spur is to be recognized as the greatest player in the world. True, after his 1984 Open Championship victory over Tom Watson, he did refer to the American as the best player but that, I feel, was Spanish courtesy (and Seve has become a very fair public speaker as a result of some 40 wins world wide). I think that since about 1982, Seve has believed that he is the best.

The European public and golf commentators and writers have long given him that status, at least jointly with Watson, but not so in the United States. On that side of the Atlantic there has been reluctance to follow suit. After all, since the end of the First World War, few individuals have challenged American supremacy with the exception perhaps of Henry Cotton in the second half of the 1930s. However, he did not play in the

States during his best years. Then, just after the Second World War, Bobby Locke had the greatest year of any overseas player on the US Tour – but even so never won a US major championship. Peter Thomson, from 1954, was for several years undoubtedly the best international player but had just one win on the US Tour. How odd that his great American victories should come in his mid-fifties on the US Senior Tour . . . And we must certainly not forget Gary Player, for so long a member of the Big Three or Four, but never thought of as the Number One, except by Gary himself.

Seve still doesn't really enjoy playing in the States. In Europe, he has been the brightest star in the firmament since that 1976 Birkdale Open Championship. In the USA, some of his experiences have left him full of resentment. He was not pleased, for instance, when he came to the last green on winning his first US tournament, the Greater Greensboro' Open in 1978, and an announcer said: 'Let's give this spic a big olé'.

A couple of years later, as Masters Champion, he was furious to be disqualified from the US Open when late on the tee. On this occasion, whoever was to blame, it was certainly not the fault of the USGA officials, who were simply applying rules intended to be the same for everyone. Later, he was distressed when leading a tournament into the last round to feel that he was being willed to lose, and lose he did.

Playing in the USA is indeed very different for Seve Ballesteros. In Europe, Australia, Japan – and wherever else he cares to appear – Ballesteros is considered just as much a Superstar as Jack Nicklaus or Tom Watson and commands the same appearance money. There is no appearance money on the US Tour and Seve is not quite the Superstar he is elsewhere. Why not, you may ask, when he has two Masters Championships and two Opens under his belt? Part of the answer is that Americans don't, as I do, give supreme status to the four majors. Being leading money winner is very important, a title Seve still needs, plus a US Open Championship or two. Of course, his appearances in the States are now problematic, following the ban placed on him by US Tour authorities in 1985. Ballesteros was supposed to play in a minimum of 15 events and didn't come close. I daresay a compromise will be reached. The US Tour needs the charisma of Ballesteros and he needs success in the States to enhance his status.

Ballesteros's tournament record in the States in the last few years is far inferior, for instance, to that of Calvin Peete. Remove his two Masters' wins from his record, and Seve is left with just the 1978 Greensboro', the 1983 Westchester Classic and the 1985 Memphis Classic. Overseas, of course, Peete has achieved nothing at all and nor have most except the very greatest American players, which is something I hope my American readers will accept. It really is difficult to play in other players' backyards and Americans are clearly no better at it than other golfing nations – except, of course, for those very few who can compete anywhere and, very importantly, don't feel uncomfortable outside the homeland.

Ballesteros's homeland in golf is not Spain but the European Tour. He starts everywhere as favourite. In the States, he is just another leading player yet, as his game matures, he has that rare ability, like Tom Watson and Jack Nicklaus, to raise his game in the major championships. This, possibly you may think is purely an attitude of mind but it's an attitude of the highest significance. When I was consistently among the top three in Britain, I went into the British Open feeling just a little inferior. As a youth, I felt if there was to be a British winner, Cotton would be the man. Later, I must admit that I felt that a bigger name than mine was bound to triumph. It would be a Palmer, Nicklaus, Thomson, Player year – but not Alliss. It all reveals a lack of belief in one and that necessary arrogance which clears the mind so that you feel you're the best around.

There's another vital factor – you have to believe that success at golf is the most important thing in the whole wide world. The club golfer who has it will win more than his due share of monthly medals; at a different level, Seve has it also. I didn't have because for me golf was just one part of my life. That doyen of golf photographers, Bert Neale, has remarked

When Seve hits full out, this is a typical finish. The 1983 US Masters

to me that if I played a rather poor shot I was apt to shrug my shoulders in a way that implied 'Well it's only a game'.

This is not a flaw that Ballesteros has. You can always see the passion when he's on the hunt, not only in a major championship but in other events as well. The stride quickens; the concentration intensifies. He's even apt to ignore his playing partner's presence. Yet he means no harm. To Ballesteros, the surge to victory blocks out everything else. Minutes after victory, he can change utterly. Just after Seve had won the 1984 British Open at St Andrews he made a little acceptance speech that was a model of its kind. There was humility (he was delighted to have beaten the greatest player in the world, Tom Watson); courtesy to his hosts (St Andrews was the greatest course in the world and the British Open was the greatest event); filial affection (his mother was there for the first time to see him win). It was all delightfully done, helped a little by the Spanish accent and, you might say, a fairly calculating and sharp brain.

Yet it had been a very different Ballesteros when he had holed a birdie putt on the last hole which made his victory inevitable. The clenched fist punched the air again and again in the seconds after it dropped. No Anglo-Saxon restraint there and why should there be? It's all part of the excitement that Ballesteros generates more than any other player since Arnold Palmer started doing just that way back in 1958.

This was the most recent of Seve's four major championships. His greatest performance, however, at this level was in the 1980 Masters. He began with a six-under-par round of 66 to share the lead. His 69 on the second day put him four ahead of the field and a third-round 68 gave him a lead of seven at thirteen under par. After the first nine in the final round the lead was ten. He then began to falter and, though inconceivable, it looked just possible that he might produce the collapse of all time, to outdo Ed Sneed's in the previous year or Curtis Strange's in 1985. Five strokes went from the 11th to the 13th and twice he was in water. For many players, such a sequence of disasters becomes uncontrollable. It can begin to seem as if every drive is going to finish deep in the trees and every downhill putt finish yards past the hole. Ballesteros played the rest of the course in one under par, which says much for his nerve and competitive toughness.

Now he thinks his swing was at its best then, rather as Jack Nicklaus believes that everything was more right with his own way back in 1960 in the Eisenhower Trophy when he went round Merion four times for a total of 269. But, like Nicklaus, and unlike so many others, Ballesteros can win when playing well below his best.

I believe that Seve is now the best player in the world and I rate him this highly partly because he is an international player with many more victories outside Europe or the States than, for example, Tom Watson. As a travelling man, he's Gary Player's successor, though I doubt he will equal the South African's international feats. As I've already mentioned,

Seve keeps his putting
stroke in good order on the
practice green at The Belfry.
Ryder Cup. 1985

Americans were a little slow to recognize his great quality. Seve's excursions into the rough in the 1979 British Open led Hale Irwin to say: 'I can't understand how a man can drive so badly and still win.' Fuzzy Zoeller, a far more generous-minded character with humour said: 'I can honestly say Daniel Boone wouldn't have found some of the territory Seve visited.' In a word, they and many other Americans thought he was just plain lucky. Opinions have changed though I doubt if the Spaniard is Hale Irwin's kind of player even now. Irwin, a superb striker, is in the Hogan mould and believes wayward shots ought to bring final retribution.

Says Ben Crenshaw, Masters' Champion in 1984: 'Seve's got shots the rest of us don't even know.' Tom Kite: 'It's like he's driving a Ferrari and the rest of us are in Chevrolets.' Tom Weiskopf: 'The most exciting player since Arnold Palmer.' Lee Trevino: 'I can talk to a fade but Seve can do it with a hook as well.' Jack Nicklaus: 'The longest hitter of a 1-iron I've ever seen.'

Yes, Seve is a player with all the talents but I don't think anyone else has so blended the most important ones to the same extent – namely power, touch, imagination, nerve and, perhaps most of all, desire.

BALLESTEROS, SEVERIANO
Born: Pedrena, Spain, 9 April 1957
Major championship victories: 1979 British Open Championship;
1980 US Masters; 1983 US Masters; 1984 British Open
Championship.
Ryder Cup player: 1979, 1983, 1985
US Tour victories (1978–84): 4
European Tour victories (1976–84): 23
Total career victories (1976–84): 38
US Tour money winnings (as a member, 1983–84): $343,592
European Tour money winnings (1974–84): £644,683
World career money winnings (1974–84): $3,101,959

THE MAJOR CHAMPIONSHIPS
1860-1985

THE MASTERS TOURNAMENT

Year	Winner	Score
1934	Horton Smith	284
1935	*Gene Sarazen	282
1936	Horton Smith	285
1937	Byron Nelson	283
1938	Henry Picard	285
1939	Ralph Guldahl	279
1940	Jimmy Demaret	280
1941	Craig Wood	280
1942	*Byron Nelson	280
1946	Herman Keiser	282
1947	Jimmy Demaret	281
1948	Claude Harmon	279
1949	Sam Snead	282
1950	Jimmy Demaret	283
1951	Ben Hogan	280
1952	Sam Snead	286
1953	Ben Hogan	274
1954	*Sam Snead	289
1955	Cary Middlecoff	279
1956	Jack Burke	289
1957	Doug Ford	282
1958	Arnold Palmer	284
1959	Art Wall	284
1960	Arnold Palmer	282
1961	Gary Player	280
1962	*Arnold Palmer	280
1963	Jack Nicklaus	286
1964	Arnold Palmer	276
1965	Jack Nicklaus	271
1966	*Jack Nicklaus	288
1967	Gay Brewer	280
1968	Bob Goalby	277
1969	George Archer	281
1970	*Billy Casper	279
1971	Charles Coody	279
1972	Jack Nicklaus	286
1973	Tommy Aaron	283
1974	Gary Player	278
1975	Jack Nicklaus	276
1976	Ray Floyd	271
1977	Tom Watson	276
1978	Gary Player	277
1979	*Fuzzy Zoeller	280
1980	Seve Ballesteros	275
1981	Tom Watson	280
1982	*Craig Stadler	284
1983	Seve Ballesteros	280
1984	Ben Crenshaw	277
1985	Bernhard Langer	282

UNITED STATES OPEN CHAMPIONSHIP

Year	Winner	Score
1895	Horace Rawlins	173–36 Holes
1896	James Foulis	152–36 Holes
1897	Joe Lloyd	162–36 Holes
1898	Fred Herd	328–72 Holes
1899	Willie Smith	315
1900	Harry Vardon	313
1901	*Willie Anderson	331
1902	Laurie Auchterlonie	307
1903	*Willie Anderson	307
1904	Willie Anderson	303
1905	Willie Anderson	314
1906	Alex Smith	295
1907	Alex Ross	302
1908	*Fred McLeod	322
1909	George Sargent	290
1910	*Alex Smith	298
1911	*Johnny McDermott	307
1912	Johnny McDermott	294
1913	*Francis Ouimet	304
1914	Walter Hagen	290
1915	Jerome Travers	297
1916	Charles Evans	286
1919	*Walter Hagen	301
1920	Ted Ray	295
1921	Jim Barnes	289
1922	Gene Sarazen	288
1923	*R. T. Jones, Jr	296
1924	Cyril Walker	297
1925	*Willie MacFarlane	291
1926	R. T. Jones, Jr	293
1927	*Tommy Armour	301
1928	*Johnny Farrell	294
1929	*R. T. Jones, Jr	294
1930	R. T. Jones, Jr	287
1931	*Billy Burke	292
1932	Gene Sarazen	286
1933	Johnny Goodman	287
1934	Olin Dutra	293
1935	Sam Parks, Jr	299
1936	Tony Manero	282
1937	Ralph Guldahl	281
1938	Ralph Guldahl	284
1939	*Byron Nelson	284
1940	*Lawson Little	287
1941	Craig Wood	284
1946	*Lloyd Mangrum	284

Year	Winner	Score
1947	*Lew Worsham	282
1948	Ben Hogan	276
1949	Cary Middlecoff	286
1950	*Ben Hogan	287
1951	Ben Hogan	287
1952	Julius Boros	281
1953	Ben Hogan	283
1954	Ed Furgol	284
1955	*Jack Fleck	287
1956	Cary Middlecoff	281
1957	*Dick Mayer	282
1958	Tommy Bolt	283
1959	Billy Casper	282
1960	Arnold Palmer	280
1961	Gene Littler	281
1962	*Jack Nicklaus	283
1963	*Julius Boros	293
1964	Ken Venturi	278
1965	*Gary Player	282
1966	*Billy Casper	278
1967	Jack Nicklaus	275
1968	Lee Trevino	275
1969	Orville Moody	281
1970	Tony Jacklin	281
1971	*Lee Trevino	280
1972	Jack Nicklaus	290
1973	Johnny Miller	279
1974	Hale Irwin	287
1975	*Lou Graham	287
1976	Jerry Pate	277
1977	Hubert Green	278
1978	Andy North	285
1979	Hale Irwin	284
1980	Jack Nicklaus	272
1981	David Graham	273
1982	Tom Watson	282
1983	Larry Nelson	280
1984	*Fuzzy Zoeller	276
1985	Andy North	279

THE BRITISH OPEN

Year	Winner	Score
1860	Willie Park	174

(The first event was open only to professionals)

Year	Winner	Score
1861	Tom Morris, Sr	163
1862	Tom Morris, Sr	163
1863	Willie Park	168
1864	Tom Morris, Sr	160
1865	Andrew Strath	162
1866	Willie Park	169
1867	Tom Morris, Sr	170

Year	Winner	Score
1868	Tom Morris, Jr	154
1869	Tom Morris, Jr	157
1870	Tom Morris, Jr	149
1871	No Championship Played	
1872	Tom Morris, Jr	166
1873	Tom Kidd	179
1874	Mungo Park	159
1875	Willie Park	166
1876	Bob Martin	176
1877	Jamie Anderson	160
1878	Jamie Anderson	157
1879	Jamie Anderson	169
1880	Bob Ferguson	162
1881	Bob Ferguson	170
1882	Bob Ferguson	171
1883	*Willie Fernie	159
1884	Jack Simpson	160
1885	Bob Martin	171
1886	David Brown	157
1887	Willie Park, Jr	161
1888	Jack Burns	171
1889	*Willie Park, Jr	155
1890	John Ball	164
1891	Hugh Kirkaldy	166

(Championship Extended from 36 to 72 Holes)

Year	Winner	Score
1892	Harold Hilton	305
1893	Willie Auchterlonie	322
1894	J. H. Taylor	326
1895	J. H. Taylor	322
1896	*Harry Vardon	316
1897	Harold Hilton	314
1898	Harry Vardon	307
1899	Harry Vardon	310
1900	J. H. Taylor	309
1901	James Braid	309
1902	Alex Herd	307
1903	Harry Vardon	300
1904	Jack White	296
1905	James Braid	318
1906	James Braid	300
1907	Arnaud Massy	312
1908	James Braid	291
1909	J. H. Taylor	295
1910	James Braid	299
1911	*Harry Vardon	303
1912	Ted Ray	295
1913	J. H. Taylor	304
1914	Harry Vardon	306
1920	George Duncan	303
1921	*Jock Hutchison	296
1922	Walter Hagen	300
1923	Arthur Havers	295
1924	Walter Hagen	301
1925	Jim Barnes	300
1926	R. T. Jones, Jr	291
1927	R. T. Jones, Jr	285
1928	Walter Hagen	292
1929	Walter Hagen	292
1930	R. T. Jones, Jr	291
1931	Tommy Armour	296
1932	Gene Sarazen	283
1933	*Denny Shute	292

Year	Winner	Score
1934	Henry Cotton	283
1935	Alfred Perry	283
1936	Alfred Padgham	287
1937	Henry Cotton	290
1938	Reg Whitcombe	295
1939	Dick Burton	290
1946	Sam Snead	290
1947	Fred Daly	293
1948	Henry Cotton	294
1949	*Bobby Locke	283
1950	Bobby Locke	279
1951	Max Faulkner	285
1952	Bobby Locke	287
1953	Ben Hogan	282
1954	Peter Thomson	283
1955	Peter Thomson	281
1956	Peter Thomson	286
1957	Bobby Locke	279
1958	*Peter Thomson	278
1959	Gary Player	284
1960	Kel Nagle	278
1961	Arnold Palmer	284
1962	Arnold Palmer	276
1963	*Bob Charles	277
1964	Tony Lema	279
1965	Peter Thomson	285
1966	Jack Nicklaus	282
1967	Roberto De Vicenzo	278
1968	Gary Player	289
1969	Tony Jacklin	280
1970	*Jack Nicklaus	283
1971	Lee Trevino	278
1972	Lee Trevino	278
1973	Tom Weiskopf	276
1974	Gary Player	282
1975	*Tom Watson	279
1976	Johnny Miller	279
1977	Tom Watson	268
1978	Jack Nicklaus	281
1979	Seve Ballesteros	283
1980	Tom Watson	271
1981	Bill Rogers	276
1982	Tom Watson	284
1983	Tom Watson	275
1984	Seve Ballesteros	276
1985	Sandy Lyle	282

PGA CHAMPIONSHIP

Year	Winner	Score
1916	Jim Barnes	1 up
1919	Jim Barnes	6 & 5
1920	Jock Hutchison	1 up
1921	Walter Hagen	3 & 2
1922	Gene Sarazen	4 & 3
1923	Gene Sarazen	1 up (38)
1924	Walter Hagen	2 up
1925	Walter Hagen	6 & 5
1926	Walter Hagen	5 & 3
1927	Walter Hagen	1 up

Year	Winner	Score
1928	Leo Diegel	6 & 5
1929	Leo Diegel	6 & 4
1930	Tommy Armour	1 up
1931	Tom Creavy	2 & 1
1932	Olin Dutra	4 & 3
1933	Gene Sarazen	5 & 4
1934	Paul Runyan	1 up (38)
1935	Johnny Revolta	5 & 4
1936	Denny Shute	3 & 2
1937	Denny Shute	1 up (37)
1938	Paul Runyan	8 & 7
1939	Henry Picard	1 up (37)
1940	Byron Nelson	1 up
1941	Vic Ghezzi	1 up (38)
1942	Sam Snead	2 & 1
1944	Bob Hamilton	1 up
1945	Byron Nelson	4 & 3
1946	Ben Hogan	6 & 4
1947	Jim Ferrier	2 & 1
1948	Ben Hogan	7 & 6
1949	Sam Snead	3 & 2
1950	Chandler Harper	4 & 3
1951	Sam Snead	7 & 6
1952	Jim Turnesa	1 up
1953	Walter Burkemo	2 & 1
1954	Chick Harbert	4 & 3
1955	Doug Ford	4 & 3
1956	Jack Burke	3 & 2
1957	Lionel Hebert	2 & 1
1958	Dow Finsterwald	276
1959	Bob Rosburg	277
1960	Jay Hebert	281
1961	*Jerry Barber	277
1962	Gary Player	278
1963	Jack Nicklaus	279
1964	Bobby Nichols	271
1965	Dave Marr	280
1966	Al Geiberger	280
1967	*Don January	281
1968	Julius Boros	281
1969	Ray Floyd	276
1970	Dave Stockton	279
1971	Jack Nicklaus	281
1972	Gary Player	281
1973	Jack Nicklaus	277
1974	Lee Trevino	276
1975	Jack Nicklaus	276
1976	Dave Stockton	281
1977	*Lanny Wadkins	282
1978	*John Mahaffey	276
1979	*David Graham	272
1980	Jack Nicklaus	274
1981	Larry Nelson	273
1982	Raymond Floyd	272
1983	Hal Sutton	274
1984	Lee Trevino	273
1985	Hubert Green	278

*   *There was a playoff*